Your First Year

How to Survive and Thrive as a New Teacher

Todd Whitaker, Madeline Whitaker,
and Katherine Whitaker

Routledge
Taylor & Francis Group

NEW YORK AND LONDON

First published 2016
by Routledge
711 Third Avenue, New York, NY 10017

and by Routledge
2 Park Square, Milton Park, Abingdon, Oxon, OX14 4RN

Routledge is an imprint of the Taylor & Francis Group, an informa business

Library of Congress Cataloging in Publication Data
Names: Whitaker, Todd, 1959- author. | Whitaker, Madeline,
author. | Whitaker, Katherine, author.
Title: Your first year : how to survive and thrive as a new teacher /
by Todd Whitaker, Madeline Whitaker, and Katherine Whitaker.
Description: New York : Routledge, 2016. | Includes
bibliographical references.
Identifiers: LCCN 2015046874 | ISBN 9781138126152 (pbk.) |
ISBN 9781315647050 (e-book)
Subjects: LCSH: First year teachers--Handbooks, manuals, etc. |
Teaching--Handbooks, manuals, etc.
Classification: LCC LB2844.1.N4 W53 2016 | DDC 371.102--dc23
LC record available at http://lccn.loc.gov/2015046874

ISBN: 978-1-138-12615-2 (pbk)
ISBN: 978-1-315-64705-0 (ebk)

Typeset in Palatino
by Saxon Graphics Ltd, Derby

Contents

eResources

This book is accompanied by two free study guides—one for practicing teachers and one for student teachers. Go to the book's product page, www.routledge.com/9781138126152. Click on the tab that says eResources and click on the study guide you'd like to read. It will begin downloading to your computer.

Meet the Authors

From left to right: Katherine, Todd, and Madeline Whitaker

Dr. Todd Whitaker has been fortunate to be able to blend his passion with his career. Recognized as a leading presenter in the field of education, his message about the importance of teaching has resonated with hundreds of thousands of educators around the world. Todd is a professor of educational leadership at Indiana State University in Terre Haute, Indiana, and he has spent his life pursuing his love of education by researching and studying effective teachers and principals.

Prior to moving into higher education he was a math teacher and basketball coach in Missouri. Todd then served as a principal at the middle school, junior high, and high school levels. He was also a middle school coordinator in charge of staffing, curriculum, and technology for the opening of new middle schools.

One of the nation's leading authorities on staff motivation, teacher leadership, and principal effectiveness, Todd has written over 40 books including the national bestseller, *What Great Teachers Do Differently*. Other titles include: *Shifting the Monkey, Dealing with Difficult Teachers, The 10 Minute Inservice, The Ball, What Great Principals Do Differently, Motivating & Inspiring Teachers,* and *Dealing with Difficult Parents.*

Todd is married to Beth, also a former teacher and principal, who is a professor of Elementary Education at Indiana State University. They are the parents of three children: Katherine, Madeline, and Harrison.

Madeline Whitaker is currently an elementary teacher in Springfield, Missouri. She was raised in Terre Haute, Indiana, and attended Vanderbilt University to pursue her undergraduate degree at the Peabody College of Education. She graduated with a Bachelor of Science Degree in Elementary Education and Child Studies. Additionally, upon graduating, she received the Dorothy J. Skeel Award for Outstanding Professional Promise in Elementary Education. After moving to Columbia to begin her teaching career, she enrolled in a degree program at the University of Missouri. She will be graduating in 2016 with her Master of Education Degree in Educational Leadership and Policy Analysis as well as her elementary and secondary principal certification.

Katherine Whitaker is currently a high school math teacher in Kansas City, Missouri. She was raised in Terre Haute, Indiana and attended the University of Missouri to pursue her dreams of teaching. In 2012, Katherine received her Bachelor of Science Degree in Secondary Mathematics Education. Her first three years in the classroom were spent at the middle school level teaching 8th grade math, algebra, and reading. She is now teaching Algebra A, Algebra I, and Algebra II Honors at the high school level. Katherine will be graduating with her Master of Science in Educational Leadership K–12 from Northwest Missouri State University in 2016 and plans on starting her doctorate in the near future.

The Most Special Profession

Congratulations! If you are reading this book, you have chosen to make a difference with your life and career. Just think about that. You have decided that you want to take your skills and abilities and help others better themselves. Wow. If you ever forget to feel goosebumps when students walk into your classroom, just remember the influence and impact you have on so many others. Every day you will make a difference. That's hopefully why you chose education and now it has become reality.

You will quickly realize that other things have also become reality. What do I do if the students stop listening to me? How do I deal with an upset parent? How can I get enough sleep? And most importantly—When do I have time to go to the bathroom?!

Every day is different. Every day is special. Every day is a challenge. But, you are up to the challenge! Of course there will be special moments that touch your heart, times you wonder what you got into, and occasions where you want to (or most likely will) cry. You knew that when you chose to be a teacher. That may be part of the reason you chose to be a teacher.

But you don't just want to be "a" teacher. You want to become "the" teacher. You want to be the teacher who inspires others because you had teachers who inspired you. You want to be the teacher who the students come and visit the next year and the ones after that. You want to be the teacher who makes a difference in the lives of the young people in your classroom. And, you know what? You can be. Now it's up to you.

You will have students who have unlimited potential. They are the ones who can change the world, invent the newest technology, maybe find a cure for cancer. It's always fun to work with students like this. Every day with them is amazing. You can even take a little credit for how smart and gifted they are. And you should.

Additionally, you will have some students who have more challenges. Maybe it is their home life, maybe it is their skill set, maybe it is their attitude. Maybe it is their fault. Maybe it isn't. These students will really be the ones to test your patience and abilities. The teachers who can reach all students are so different than the ones who can reach some students. And though it may be frustrating at times, when you see that glint in the eyes when there is new understanding, a smile on their face when they finally catch onto a concept, or a newfound dedication because they realize they can do it after all, you will realize that you really have chosen the right profession.

You will never forget the students you have your first year. Others may fade in and out of your memory, but these students will never leave your memory and they will never leave your heart. There is something special about your very first group. They are unforgettable. And you want to make sure you are the kind of teacher who is unforgettable too. That is the reason we wrote *Your First Year*. Strap in, because it will be the ride of your life. You will go on the most energizing and exhilarating journey. It will be like nothing you could imagine and everything you could hope for all at the same time. Thank you for choosing to teach. Thank you for choosing to make a difference. Thank you for choosing to matter.

How to Use This Book

Your First Year is designed to be usable in multiple ways. You can pick it up and read it cover to cover while you are still in college or use it as reference guide during your first year of teaching. Hopefully it can provide a guide for you as you anticipate things you want to have prepared before the first day of school, as well as be used in a stand-alone fashion so that if you are facing a particular challenge (or crisis!) you can immediately turn to that as a resource or refresher.

Your First Year is written for elementary, middle school, and high school teachers, providing you with multiple examples in differing contexts. We have attempted to include the specificity needed so that you will know precisely how to set up expectations, communicate with students and adults, and prepare your classroom. We are also aware that every reader has different backgrounds and experiences. Some of you have always enjoyed school, were raised in a family with educators, and have or will student teach with a master teacher. Others of you may not have had such opportunities. Either way, this book will help you navigate your way to a successful first year.

It may seem that a disproportionate amount of the book is centered on student/classroom management. We have learned from new teachers that this is the number one concern they have heading into their first year and the number one challenge they face during the first year (and sometimes many beyond that). We felt it is essential to provide a richness in the area to support new teachers in what many consider to be the most challenging aspect of teaching. If a teacher has good classroom management they still may not be effective, but if they do not have good classroom management they can never be effective.

We also wanted to provide some guidance in working with adults in and outside your school. Finding peers who you can share with and learn from can be so rewarding. Being able to effectively communicate with and receive support from parents is very valuable. But at times we may work or interact with adults who may not always have an altruistic purpose. Making sure that we navigate these, at times challenging, waters can be an important part of enjoying our first year in a school.

Lastly, we would love to hear from you! If you would like to share your stories with us and other readers on Twitter, just add the hashtag #YourFirstYear. It will be a chance to learn, laugh, and grow together. Enjoy the book and have a wonderful First Year.

Section I

Before the Students Arrive: Structure, Structure, Structure

1

Setting Up and Organizing Your Classroom

Teaching is a complicated profession, and there are many facets to being an outstanding educator. As a beginning teacher, however, it is imperative to have one main focus for the first few weeks before and after school begins: managing the classroom. In a large-scale meta-analysis, Wang, Haertel, and Walberg (1993) studied the effect of a variety of influences on student achievement, and they found classroom management to have the greatest impact. Also, research has shown that the majority of teachers consider discipline issues the most stressful part of their job (Wasicsko & Ross, 1994). In your first year, there are many things that you won't know or you won't get right—but your structure and procedures should not be one of them.

> In your first year, there are many things that you won't know or you won't get right—but your structure and procedures should not be one of them.

How spacious, attractive, or modern the classroom, portable, or pod that you will get the keys to is out of your hands, but what you turn it into is entirely in your control. Many different researchers and educational experts, including Fred Jones in *Tools for Teaching: Discipline, Instruction, Motivation, 3rd Edition* (2013), defend the critical importance of classroom arrangement. While you are setting up (and possibly cleaning up from how it was left after the previous year), you will need to think about two major aspects of your classroom: the furniture and the materials.

Furniture

With regard to furniture, it is important to focus on classroom flow, functionality, and structure. Many of the basic classroom management issues can be addressed even before students enter the classroom by making sure the furniture is set up in a functional way (Jones, 2013). Thus, begin by thinking through these major questions: How many students will you have? Do you have enough desks or tables? What configuration will help you be most successful from day one? Your class size will largely determine how your class will be set up. Let's look at two different examples of teachers who arranged their classroom before the first day of school.

Ms. George is a middle school science teacher with 30–35 students in each class. She was placed in one of the smallest classrooms in the school, and this, paired with her large class sizes, limits her options on how to design the space. She is also a bit nervous about managing a class that large, so she is looking for a classroom set-up that will be beneficial as she introduces her classroom expectations and procedures with students. The best option for Ms. George is to start the year off with her desks in evenly spaced and orderly rows. This will allow movement between desks to be seamless and help limit student interaction. Even though Ms. George really wants her desks in groups so students can collaborate during labs, she knows that she can introduce a different desk arrangement at any time. Her main goal at the start of the year is seamless implementation of structure and order. Once she establishes her procedures and routines, she then can move the desks into groups because it is always easier to become less structured instead of more structured.

Mr. Grant is an elementary teacher with 25 students, and he has a fairly large classroom. Because of this, he can be more flexible in how he designs his set-up. He feels confident about placing his desks in groups because most of the whole-class instruction will be done on the carpet. Thus, he decides to group the 25 desks into pods of five, keep the area in front of the board open for his carpet, and then reserve the back corner by the window for the classroom library. Even though Mr. Grant has more flexibility to be creative, his main focus is still flow, functionality, and structure—it just looks dissimilar to Ms. George's because his classroom, students, needs, and comfort level are different.

When you are setting up your classroom furniture, the final, and maybe the most important thing to think through is making sure that you will be able to monitor all students at all times, no matter where you are instructing from. If Ms. George has one desk hidden behind a file cabinet, or if Mr. Grant's reading nook is nestled behind the technology center, both teachers have set up a situation that could turn sour quickly. There would be places that students could go in the classroom and be "hidden." Now, there is a chance that Mr. Grant and Ms. George could have a class of perfect angels who would never ever take advantage of those "hidden gems," but as a new teacher we would not take that risk. It would be much easier to be proactive about those possible issues than to be reactive and have to deal with the behavior later.

Materials

The second aspect of classroom set-up and organization is the materials that you will be working with. Make sure that necessary and regularly used materials are easily accessible, while less-frequented materials are stored away in an organized fashion that allows you to retrieve them when the time comes. What are things that you and your students will need on a day-to-day basis? Pencils? Notebooks? Textbooks? What are things that you and your students may not need as regularly, but should still be accessible? Scissors? Calculators? Math manipulatives? It is also likely that you will end up with materials that you have absolutely no clue what to do with—like the previous curriculum guides. Feel free to ask your teammates or administrators what to do with the items. If they tell you to keep them, then put them somewhere that will be out of the way since they won't need to be accessed regularly.

When Ms. Smith, a 3rd grade teacher, was preparing her classroom, she made sure each student had a dry erase board and a clipboard in his or her seat pocket because in her mind those were going to be used regularly. She placed binders, however, in their locker cubbies, because those would probably be used less frequently. When it came to notebooks, she was entirely unsure if she would use them at all at the beginning of the year, so she put them neatly in a cabinet that she could easily reach when the time was right.

Although Mr. Jenkins is a high school English teacher, he too thought through placement of materials. He knew that most students would come in on day 1 with a spiral notebook, but he has many extra near his desk just in case. He also placed spare sharpened pencils in a cup on his desk so students could get one if they forgot, but also placed a sign-out sheet to keep track of them so at the end of the period he could collect those that he lent out. Finally, on the cabinets below his window, he stacked up the textbooks by class, and had them organized in number order so they were ready to be handed out efficiently.

By preparing as much as you can prior to students arriving, you increase the likelihood of success when school starts. One of the best places to start this preparation is with your furniture and materials. Once the students arrive, this planning minimizes the time you will have to deal with things other than what is most important: students and teaching.

> **By preparing as much as you can prior to students arriving, you increase the likelihood of success when school starts.**

2

Developing Your Procedures

While you are organizing your classroom and preparing for the year, you also need to think extensively about classroom procedures and expectations. These are the basic routines that you and students will use to help the classroom "run," almost like a well-oiled machine. Research has shown that procedures are a critical aspect of preventative effective classroom management that positively affects students' learning and behavior (Marzano et al., 2005). Thinking deeply about procedures in a proactive manner can be a huge make-or-break with regard to student management and overall classroom climate.

The tighter your procedures are, the less misbehavior will occur and the calmer and more productive the environment will be. Listed below are many of the common classroom procedures that teachers of a variety of grades must think through:

> **The tighter your procedures are, the less misbehavior will occur and the calmer and more productive the environment will be.**

◆ Pencils: How will students get them? How will they get sharpened? What if a student forgets one? What if the student needs an eraser?

◆ Notebooks/textbooks: Will students come into the classroom each day with them? If not, how will you get them handed out each day? What if a student comes one day without them?

◆ Homework: Where will it be turned in or how will you collect it? How will you return it to the students after grading?

◆ Late work: How will students learn about what information they missed? What system will you use so they have access to the make-up work?

◆ Bathroom: How often can students use the bathroom? How will they let you know that they need to use the bathroom? Will you need to keep track of how many times a student has used the bathroom?

◆ Technology: How will classroom technology be stored? If portable, how will it be distributed to students? Will devices need to be charged overnight?

◆ Phones, tablets, personal devices: What is your school's policy? When are the times students can access them? When are the times they should be put away?

◆ Entering the classroom: Should students remove hats? Are they to be quiet? Should they go straight to their seats? What work should they get started on?

◆ Exiting the classroom: Will you dismiss students? Do they leave when the bell rings? Is there a line order they must learn? Should they line up quietly?

In addition to overall basic procedures that apply to almost all teachers, there will also be some that apply to just you and your classroom. For example, 1st grade teachers will need to think through where their students will store their backpacks and lunches after they walk into the classroom, while 11th grade chemistry teachers will need to think through how students will retrieve and use the beakers for experiments. Take time to walk through your classroom and think through your day—make a list of what procedures you should be proactive about.

On the next page is a more extensive list of possible things that will require procedures. Although this may not be an exhaustive list of everything you will need to prepare for, it should be a strong base that can help you begin to process your procedural expectations. Keep in mind that once students arrive, adjustments will most likely need to be made based on your students and unanticipated situations. Thus, use this list to prepare as best you can, knowing that there will be mid-flight corrections.

Kleenexes
Students asking questions
Checking out books from the school library and/or your classroom library
Eating food in the classroom
Storing and distributing materials that may not be used daily (crayons, colored pencils, scissors, glue, etc.)
Taking attendance
Fire drill
Beginning of the day/period routines
End of the day/period routines
Tornado drill
Lost items
Throwing away trash and/or recycling
Classroom jobs
Unfinished work
Technology availability and utilization
Earthquake drill
Late work
Make-up work
Seating arrangement
Students who are tardy
Acceptable noise levels
Talking and participating during lessons
Getting into/choosing groups
Lockdown drill
Sudden illness
Dismissal

This list of things you will need procedures for may seem overwhelming at first. Fortunately, there may be others who have already solved this issue for you. For example, your school may already have procedures for walking down the hallway, checking out books from the library, and even emergency drills. For others, you may ask a mentor teacher, a trusted colleague, or even look for different ideas on the Internet.

Always remember that it is better to be over prepared than under prepared when it comes to procedures. As a matter of fact, it is almost impossible to be over prepared. For example, if you are unsure of whether or not you will need to keep track of when students use the bathroom, be safe and start out with a system. If you find

> **Always remember that it is better to be over prepared than under prepared when it comes to procedures.**

out that it is a non-issue, then you can taper away from that structure. If it turns out to be a huge help, though, then you will be very grateful that you began that structure on day 1! As mentioned previously, it is much easier to loosen structures after school has begun than to tighten them once the students have arrived.

3

Developing Your Rules

A final part of classroom preparation is thinking through your classroom rules. There is a significant amount of research that describes the importance of establishing clear rules (Marzano et al., 2005). Rules are different from procedures because they are broader, generally pertain to student behavior and character, and have some sort of consequence when they are broken. This part of preparation is critical because your rules will be something that you enforce every day, thus you want to use them to cultivate the type of classroom that you desire.

Some teachers choose to have a set of classroom rules posted on the wall right when students walk in the first day. Some prefer to form the rules together as a class to build student ownership of them. Others may just use the school rules that students are already familiar with, so they only need to be addressed during the first day of class. Certain master teachers, especially secondary ones, do not even have explicit rules or expectations posted in their classroom—but they are clearly written in their heads. No matter which type of teacher you are, make sure that *you* have a clear vision of what you want the rules to be.

> No matter which type of teacher you are, make sure that *you* have a clear vision of what you are wanting the rules to be.

A teacher's rules should represent his or her core philosophy, and they should drive the climate of the classroom. Even teachers who don't consciously have a set of classroom rules still have them subconsciously buried in their brains on a daily basis. As a first year teacher, you won't be able to define classroom rules as clearly as the master teacher down the hallway is able to do. Thus, you must think through exactly which ones you need based on what type of classroom you want to run.

Always remind yourself that rules, when implemented effectively, represent the philosophy of the classroom teacher and drive the tone of the classroom. What kind of climate do you want to build in your classroom? Which rules will help you do that most effectively? What are your personal non-negotiables? Also, do not be afraid to include non-traditional rules like "Take chances." We call these "culture-building" rules. The term "culture-building" comes from the motive behind the rule. Most rules are put in place to let students know what behavior is not appropriate. Some rules, however, can be put in place to build a certain positive classroom environment. For example, "Take chances" helps build a classroom full of tenacious students who can picture success, whereas "Finish all work" does not build motivation, and may not even be a realistic rule for struggling students to follow.

On the next page is a list of example classroom rules. Feel free to go through this list and critically reflect upon which ones you want to use. Keep in mind, whatever rule you put in place, you will have to enforce it on a *consistent* and *daily* basis. If you feel discomfort with any rule you are contemplating, it may better to not include it, especially at the very start of your first year. Wasicisko and Ross (1994) summarize this idea nicely: "To avoid the pitfalls of inconsistency, mean what you say, and when you say it, follow through" (p. 64).

Keep in mind, whatever rule you put in place, you will have to enforce it on a *consistent* and *daily* basis.

As you look through these rules, you may be tempted to create a large list that details every possible misbehavior you can imagine.

Having too many rules that are too specific can become extremely cumbersome to a teacher, and actually be counterproductive. Thus, when developing rules, choose only a few, and whenever possible, word them in ways that let students know what you want them to do, instead of what you do not want them to do.

- ◆ Be safe
- ◆ Complete all assignments
- ◆ One person at a time
- ◆ Be on time
- ◆ Keep your hands to yourself
- ◆ Be prepared
- ◆ Raise your hand before talking
- ◆ Be a risk-taker
- ◆ Use technology appropriately
- ◆ Respect others and their property

Here are two examples of teachers who went through the process of thinking through their rules. We hope these will help guide you in your own brainstorming.

Ms. Potter is a 1st grade teacher trying to think through her classroom rules. She understands that 1st graders are not going to be very independent, so she needs to make her rules fairly specific. Her first rule that she knows she wants is "Respect your class-mates and teacher" because her mentor teacher had that as a rule, and being able to reference it when students were having issues was very helpful. She then began to write down, "Raise your hand to leave your seat," but realized that may not be a great rule for her class. She is planning on doing literacy stations that will require students to be able to move independently as she is doing small-group instruction, thus having to raise their hand to move stations or get materials does not make sense. After giving much thought to what rules would best serve her classroom, she ended with this list of four things she felt were essential: 1. Respect your classmates and teacher. 2. Listen quietly while others are talking. 3. Follow directions the first time. 4. Change tasks quietly.

Mr. Wilson is preparing for his first year as a 12th grade AP English teacher at a private school. He knows that he is going to get some of the best students in the school, but he also does not want students to come into a classroom without any expectations. Thus, instead of having classroom rules that pertain to behavior, he is going to choose some that are more academically driven because that is probably where issues will pop up. He also remembers how dull AP English was for him in high school, so he wants to include one "Culture-building" rule to set the tone for the type of climate he wants to cultivate. After carefully considering what students will need to do to be successful in his classroom, he decided on three basic rules that he will introduce on the first day: 1. Be prepared for class every day. 2. Participate in classroom discussions. 3. Be a literary risk-taker!

Now, take some time to come up with potential rules of your own. Write them down in a notebook or list them in a mobile device or computer. You will need a physical list to refer to as we assist you in reflecting, processing, and adjusting your preliminary rules.

As you take time to filter through your potential rules, reflect on these three questions:

◆ Do you feel comfortable consistently enforcing the rules you have chosen?
◆ Do you need to make varied rules for different classes that you teach?
◆ Did you choose rules that you think your students will also be able to take ownership of?

These three questions address the legitimacy of the rule as well as the critical student buy-in. It is important to make sure that the rules you choose are ones you feel comfortable consistently enforcing, thus there is regular follow-through each time the rule is violated. For example, when you choose a rule, such as "Raise your hand to speak," would you feel comfortable enforcing it even though you have regular full-class debates? If not, the rule may eventually become meaningless. Instead, you could choose the rule, "Listen respectfully while others are talking," since that is something that is appropriate at all times, and something that is not followed if a student blurts disruptively while you are teaching. Additionally, do not be afraid to have different rules and expectations for different times of the day or even varied activities. For example, you may want to use the rule "Raise Your Hand to Speak" during whole-class instruction but not throughout the rest of the class period or day. To implement this, you could post a sign that reads "Instructional Time" or "Teacher Time" when you need students to raise their hands for permission to speak. Once the whole-group lesson is completed, you can take the sign down and return to your normal classroom routines.

The purpose of the final reflective question was to remind you that choosing rules your students will buy into will help them feel empowered—which is an essential aspect of building a positive classroom climate. If you simply tell them that the rule is "Raise your hand to speak," without offering any genuine rationale or explanation of why, their motivation to follow the rule will be lower. This is why some teachers choose to create a set of rules with their students. However, many effective managers choose their own rules, and if you do this, just remember it may be beneficial to share your reasoning behind these choices. This may help diminish the tendency of less effective teachers to use the "because I said so" mentality. For example, if you had the rule "Raise Your Hand to Speak," tell students you chose it by connecting it to their own lives. Remind them of how frustrating it can be when you are trying to share a thought or opinion, but people jump in before you are complete. These types of explanations and connections can solidify critical buy-in of the rules and prevent defiance later.

Finally, if you are ever worried that your rules might be thought of as too basic or elementary you can go ahead and start with them and see how it goes. Later in the book, we discuss ways to slightly adjust or even dramatically alter rules and procedures that turn out to be uncomfortable for you, or inappropriate for your students.

4

Classroom Management: Prepare Your Mindset

For almost all first year teachers, classroom management is the make-or-break. As mentioned previously, this is where some of the biggest struggles come from for all teachers—yet this does not need to be the case for you. What we have done so far is establish a foundation to prepare you for classroom management. We have given you the tools to prepare your classroom set-up, procedures, and rules. Now is the time to think about your students as more than just students. They are real people, and you must now consider how you will teach them to work together, be respectful, follow directions, and simply behave. What will truly be the largest predictor of your success as a manager is a combination of three things—relationships, high and specific expectations, and consistency.

Relationships

We are going to work you through a simple metaphor of building and maintaining a house to help you think through what classroom management looks like, and to do this we will begin with relationships. Relationships with your students are like the strong and solid foundation of a house. When built correctly, this type of foundation is strong on the 70-degree-and-sunny days, and will continue to maintain on the severe-thunderstorm-warning days. This is just like your classroom. When relationships are built correctly, those bonds will be there to help you celebrate on your best days, and also to keep your classroom cohesive on your worst. According to Emmer and Saborine (2015), "building positive relationships with students should be a primary focus of preventative efforts" when it comes to classroom management (p. 27). As cited by Emmer and Saborine (2015), research has shown that positive student–teacher relationships not only positively affect student attitudes and learning (Cornelius-White, 2007; Roorda, Koomen, Spilt, & Oort, 2001), but also have direct ties to teacher burnout and overall job satisfaction (Chang, 2009; Friedman, 2006; Klassen & Chiu, 2010).

Thus, when planning on how to build these critical relationships, make sure that your core philosophies are in the correct place. You must come into teaching with a genuine belief that every student matters and every student has the capacity to learn. According to research published by Carol S. Dweck in her book *Mindset* (2006), having growth mindset, or the belief that all students are capable of cognitive growth and development, directly affects your students' academic growth and performance. If you do not believe in your students, they will realize it, and consequently not fulfill their unknown potential. Think about it—would you really want to be taught by someone who did not think you were worth their while or could actually learn anything? Of course not! You may even encounter teachers at your school who have these beliefs, but do not let them undermine what you know in your heart (and what research says) is right.

You must come into teaching with a genuine belief that every student matters and every student has the capacity to learn.

Now, what does "building relationships" actually look like? You may have heard over and over again how important it is, but are still unsure as to what it looks like. There is a chance you have or are planning on looking up blogs and asking around about how to build relationships with students. Some people may tell you about different "get to know you" games to do on the first day of school, so you will choose three because you want to have great relationships with your students. After that first day, your students will have fun with the games, and you may learn interesting facts about them, but your job is far from over. Building relationships is in fact much more than "find someone who …" games. Every single time you interact with a student is a chance to build that relationship, from the first day to the last, and if you always focus on making sure students feel heard and cared about, you will be right on your way to building those crucial bonds.

Below are some basic ways that strong teachers are able to build relationships with students in their classroom:

♦ Greet students at the door each morning or class period with a smile, letting the students know you are happy they are there
♦ Regularly celebrate student achievements (could be a simple high-five, or a special conversation)
♦ Show students respect by never yelling or using sarcasm
♦ Ask students questions about their lives
♦ Listen to stories they tell
♦ Leave a private note on a student's desk pointing out something he or she did well, or something you appreciate about him or her
♦ Call home to help parents join in on the celebration of their child
♦ Remind them that you care about them each day before they leave your class

As you notice, each example is a simple and quick way to help students feel heard and cared about. No matter the age and grade level of students you work with, building bonds is a critical element of being effective in the classroom. This is just a small list that, over many years of teaching, will continuously grow and flourish. We would recommend putting a star by one to three of the strategies in the list as a reminder for ways that you can build relationships during the first weeks of school. Slowly, these will become natural and you can add on more and more to your repertoire. Always remind yourself that every single interaction is a chance to build that bond, so take every moment of your day seriously.

High and Specific Expectations

Now that you have an idea of how to build relationships, we must discuss the importance of high and specific behavioral expectations. Returning back to our house-building metaphor, we learned that relationships provide the strong foundation. Now, it is actually time to build the house itself. This is the house that you will see every day—the one that you will live in. Thus, just like you wanted to have a strong foundation to build upon, you also want a solid, functional, and livable house. So what would a solid, functional, and livable classroom look like? Would it have kindergarteners crawling all over the ground while you are teaching an important literacy lesson? Would it have 10th graders having a conversation about last night's party when they are supposed to be analyzing poetry? Of course not! This is why having high and specific behavioral expectations is an additional aspect of strong behavior management skills.

According to Bridget Hamre and Robert Pianta (2006), it is critical for schools and teachers to maintain high behavioral expectations to go along with positive teacher–student relationships. Even if you do not end up in a setting where these assumptions are school-wide, you are the person who makes expectations in your classroom. If you do not expect kindergarteners to sit quietly during a lesson—then they won't. If you do not expect your 10th graders to

> **You are the person who makes expectations in your classroom.**

stay focused on a task—then they won't. Make sure that you are the teacher who expects your students to behave their best, and explains explicitly what that looks like, so that you and the students know the difference between right and wrong.

In the previous sections about procedures and rules, you thought through and chose what your procedures and rules will be. Now, we want to make sure that you also have high expectations of how those procedures and rules will be followed. Mr. Johnson and Mrs. Logan are both 8th grade social studies teachers in an inner-city school. They both teach the same curriculum, serve the same clientele, and even use the same procedure where students are allowed to get pencils from the "sharpened pencil" container any time during the lesson.

Mr. Johnson came to the team meeting one day frustrated about how many issues he had been having with students getting pencils. Mrs. Logan was surprised at his concerns because she, in fact, loved the procedure they had decided on and was ready to tell the entire school about it at their next faculty meeting. What caused this huge disparity in success? The major differences were the level of expectation for the procedures and how these were communicated to the class.

When Mr. Johnson introduced the procedure, he simply told students that they could get up and get a new pencil at any time. Mrs. Logan also told students that they could get up and get a new pencil at any time, but included that they must do it quietly, and take a specific route behind all of the desks so it will cause as little distraction as possible. That major difference (along with Mrs. Logan's ability to enforce the proper behavior, which will be addressed in the "classroom management" section) was that Mrs. Logan had higher expectations as to how this procedure should be completed. From day one, her students knew that they were entirely free to get pencils whenever they needed them, but they had to do it in a specific way that would prevent any disturbance. Mr. Johnson's students, however, simply knew they could get a pencil at any time. Both classes were following the expectation correctly—but the teachers chose to have different levels of how they expected the procedure to be completed.

Now that you understand the difference between normal expectations, high expectations, and how to clearly communicate these, think through the procedures and rules you have chosen, and decide the nitty-gritty details of what your expectations are going to be. How will you want your students to enter the classroom? Chatting with their classmates, or quietly going straight to work? How will you want your students to react when someone gets a question wrong? Laughing and mocking the student, or celebrating their courageous attempt? Also, will you rely on the inherent understanding of students to know the difference between right and wrong or will you teach and model appropriate ways to deal with potential situations? The level of expectation that you have and how you explicitly state it to students will be a deciding factor in your students' behaviour. Remember, this is the house you will live in on a daily basis, so make sure it is one that will last for the long haul.

Consistency

Picture this: You now have your house built. It is built on a sturdy foundation, and looks beautiful with its brick exterior and welcoming front porch. You absolutely love living in it, and you cannot imagine moving out. Then one day, you have a leaky faucet in your upstairs bathroom. You think to yourself, "Hmm … this is just a leaky faucet. Not a huge issue—I will fix it later." In two weeks, you now have hard-water build-up around your leaky faucet. Even though you are disappointed, you still think of that issue as minor, and decide you will get back to it another time. After one month, you walk into a back room of your house that you rarely visit, and find a wet mark on the ceiling. You run upstairs and discover that your leaky faucet has more issues than you thought—and now you are left dealing with broken plumbing, a ruined floor, and even a damaged ceiling! In that moment, you realize that you should have just fixed that leaky faucet when you first found it.

This story continues our metaphor of the house that we build. The foundation of the house is the relationships, and the actual house we live in each day is the expectations that we have. Now, how do we keep the house running smoothly? Regular basic upkeep. In the classroom, this regular upkeep represents consistency. Consistency applies to both relationships and expectations, because as you know you must take regular care of the foundation of a house as well as the interior of the house itself!

Mrs. Davis was a first year teacher, and had successfully made it to mid-October. Even though the first couple weeks of teaching were a bit rocky, she felt like she had found her groove about halfway through September. She felt like she had gotten to know her students well through many of the beginning-of-the-year activities, and she also had worked hard to explain procedures and rules—and it seemed like the students had understood all of them. Recently, however, her students had begun to act like they did at the beginning of the year. They were talking back to her when she asked them to fix certain behaviors and they were even starting to sharpen pencils with the loud electric pencil sharpener while she was teaching! Mrs. Davis knew she had taught students what she wanted, but it seemed like all of a sudden her classroom morphed into something she was not comfortable with or proud of.

Even though Mrs. Davis had obviously worked hard building relationships and had successfully explained all of the procedures, there was one major gap in her practice: consistency. She had gotten so comfortable with the success that she had achieved, she failed at consistently continuing to do two things: maintain expectations and build relationships.

In situations like these, it is important to remember that students typically do not leap from ideal behavior directly to an out-of-control action. It is much more likely that students make a subtle step-by-step slide downward that is allowed to occur. What most likely happened was that Mrs. Davis had a rule that students must raise their hand before talking, and it initially seemed pretty simple and easily enforced. However, one day a very responsible student, James, interrupted excitedly but then quickly corrected himself by saying, "Sorry." Then another student with a sharp wit added something that caused a good laugh to ripple across the classroom. These soon became part of the norm and gradually other students chimed in with comments that were sometimes not quite as clever. Eventually, Mrs. Davis decided that this was enough and addressed the students by reminding them of the rule in an exasperated and harsh fashion. The students felt like—and even proclaimed that—others were doing it also! Sadly, they were right. What happened was that Mrs. Davis had lost her consistent enforcement of the rule, which caused it to gradually chip away and eventually totally disappear.

So what could she have done differently to continue her beginning-of-the-year success? Instead of ignoring the interruption the first time, Mrs. Davis could have addressed it in a variety of ways. She could have used proximity as a reminder to James, tap him on the shoulder to redirect him, or even taken the time to have a private conversation with him. As long as she addressed it appropriately, she would be maintaining that nice house.

Mrs. Davis also should have reflected upon her relationship with James. Although she knew she had built a bond with him quickly, had she worked hard to maintain it? Had she greeted him *consistently*? Complimented his hard work *consistently*? Reminded him that she cared for and believed in him *consistently*? After thinking, she realized that she only did this during the first couple of weeks, and had forgotten to continue the practice once things got comfortable. When students do not feel like you care, it is difficult for them to act like they care.

As mentioned previously, the purpose of this house metaphor was to set up your mindset for effective classroom management. As you think through your plans and begin your school year, never forget the three critical aspects of the type of classroom that you want to create: relationships, high and specific expectations, and consistency. No matter what roadblocks and difficulties occur, remember to always reflect upon which of the three criteria you are missing. Are you forgetting to build the strong structure of your house by requiring high expectations? Are you avoiding calling the plumber for the minor leak in the kitchen? Or have you invested in a weak foundation that is causing your entire house to collapse? By using this metaphor, you are now equipped with the proper mindset to prepare for managing your classroom.

Can We Maintain Consistency, But Still Change?

Consistency does not mean that teachers cannot change their expectations. This may seem like a contradiction, but actually isn't at all. All teachers do this, especially good ones. If the students in your class have demonstrated the maturity and ability to sharpen their pencil on their own and through the increased implementation of technology in your classroom seldom even need pencils, altering your rule or the enforcement of it is a natural step to having a more sensible expectation. However, if you start to move in a certain direction, do not, when your patience is more limited, overreact by dramatically adjusting back to where you were. It is unfair to the students and will damage the relationships you have worked so hard to establish.

Finally, it is important to remember that many first year teachers (especially special education teachers!) will most likely have students with IEPs (Individualized Education Programs) and 504 plans in their classrooms. Even with this diversity, you can still have basic classroom procedures and expectations that all students must follow, but you may have to change them based on those students' capabilities. In situations like these, fair is not always equal, but you must have some structures in place to make sure that you can have a manageable classroom that students can succeed in. Also remember that just because a student has an IEP and a 504 does not mean that you can make excuses for him or her. That actually does a disservice to those students because then they get comfortable performing at below their potential. Thus, when planning the necessary adaptations for these students, do not begin to make excuses just because they are in the expectational education category. Never forget what was mentioned earlier: All students matter and all students have a capacity to learn. Do not let your excuses prevent your students from living up to their full potential.

No matter the grade level or subject you will be teaching, your prepared mindset is critical in dictating how successful you will be in managing your classroom. You need strong relationships to solidify your foundation, high and clear expectations to make your classroom functional and livable, and consistency to provide the necessary upkeep. These three requirements can help you make a safe and comfortable classroom that you can call home.

When Students Follow
the Rules ... Or Don't

Now that you have a clear mindset of what you need to have successful classroom management, it is time to think about two critical questions:

1. What will you do if students follow the rules?
2. What will you do if students do not follow the rules?

Notice we are not talking about students following a procedure, which will be addressed in the next section. We are talking about rules—those few behaviors that you are going to require your students to uphold at all times in your classroom. Classroom management is all about prevention, because there is no perfect reaction. Thus, thinking about your answer to question 1 is most important because that is what you should rely on most of each day. One of the most essential factors in influencing student behavior is not determining what to do when students misbehave. It is determining what to do when students behave. In every class the majority of the students, the majority of the time, behave. Now, the question to ask is "What can we do to continually increase the number of students and percentage of time that this is happening?"

There are many different strategies that teachers use to reinforce positive behavior and give consequences for negative behavior, and there are a variety of philosophies behind each of the strategies. As a first year teacher, you do not have a proven philosophy yet, simply because you have not had your first class! Thus, you need to focus on a strategy that does two things:

◆ Focuses on positive reinforcement of good behaviors
◆ Provides consequences for inappropriate behavior

No matter the management structure you choose, some sort of reinforcement of good behavior must be at its core. Without this, whatever actions you take when students misbehave will become totally irrelevant. As a teacher, you should focus on positive behaviors the large majority of the time that you are managing your classroom. This is a way that you can build your warm classroom climate because you will be managing student behavior in a positive way. Additionally, it is actually easier for teachers to effectively manage a classroom using positive reinforcement (versus punishment) because punishment works best when implemented consistently, whereas positive reinforcement is effective even when used intermittently (Maag, 2001). Thus, when you are analyzing different strategies you think of or find, always think about how you could make these focus on the positive, because an affirmative and supportive classroom climate is one you will be proud of and one that your students will thrive in.

Although you want to generally focus on positive actions, it is also important for you to have planned consequences that you can put in your "tool belt." To be a successful classroom manager, you must hold students accountable for their inappropriate actions. Without a plan for what you will do when students are not acting appropriately, you will run the risk of losing control of your classroom quickly. These consequences can be ones that require you to take something away from a student (e.g., take away a ticket that you give for good behavior, or take away one minute from their passing period), impart something onto a student (e.g., no recess, or lunch detention), or simply just a way for students to take a break ("cool down" seat or let them go take a quick drink to blow off steam).

Different teachers will use different consequence systems, but what is important is that yours follows four criteria: consistent, reasonable, fair, and always focused on your "end goal"—for the student to have better behavior next time. For example, you may be an elementary teacher who takes away a student's point if they break a rule, or you may be a secondary teacher who makes a student come back to class during their lunch period to discuss what happened. No matter what you choose, you must prepare to do these four things to have a successful consequence system:

1. **Implement it consistently.** As mentioned previously, consistency is one of the critical aspects of a successfully managed classroom. Do you remember the quote, "Mean what you say, and when you say it, follow through" (Wasicisko & Ross, 1994, p. 64)? This is when you must put that quote into action. When a student misbehaves, you must give the consequence any time a student breaks one of your rules. If students see that you only *sometimes* provide a consequence, then the rules in your classroom will quickly become meaningless, and potentially become more harmful than good.

2. **Be fair, but also remember that fair does not always mean equal.** Although giving a consequence every single time a rule is broken is critical, you also must consider the behavior and the student when giving a consequence. Jim Fay and David Funk summarize this concept nicely in their book *Teaching with Love and Logic* (1995): "Fair is not identical treatment, but rather, giving what is needed" (p. 100).

   First, know that you do not have to give the exact same consequence every single time a rule is broken. Let's say that a student, La'Tavion, broke the rule "Respect your classmates" by talking while another student was talking, whereas Ja'Shauna broke the exact same rule by tripping a student as he walked to his seat. Although both students broke the same rule, the consequences may be different because the behavior was different.

   It is also important to understand who you will be giving the consequence to. Let's say that Mariana and Jose both broke the rule "Follow directions the first time." One plan of action you may take is to give each student the same consequence *if you think that would be effective*. With that said, you could also make them different depending on what will motivate them or even depending on if either of them had misbehaved previously that day. If it is Mariana's second or third time not "following directions the first time," while it is only Jose's first, their consequences *should* be different, because it would not be fair if they were the same!

3. **Be reasonable about the consequence—i.e., the punishment should fit the crime.** Consequences could range from a simple tap on the shoulder to a student being sent to a "buddy room," but what consequence you implement entirely depends on the severity of the misbehavior. It is essential for the consequence to reflect the student's behavior, and not your current mood. For example, if the student broke a rule about raising his hand to speak once, it would not make sense to then make the student sit in lunch detention for an entire week. That consequence is too extreme for the level of and motive behind the misbehavior. There is a good chance that the student did not blurt out on purpose. On the other hand, if you have a student who shoved another student and your consequence is a tap on the shoulder, that would also not make sense. Shoving a student is very serious since it compromises the safety of the classroom, thus you would need to provide a consequence serious enough to reflect the behavior. In that situation, the consequence needs to let the student know that his or her behavior was absolutely unacceptable. You need to make sure they understand the severity of the situation because they endangered another student. The higher your expectations are, the better their behavior will be. Keep in mind, however, that every time you send a student to the office,

> It is essential for the consequence to reflect the student's behavior, and not your current mood.

it gives away a bit of your power. This does not mean you should never use the office to help provide you support. Just be thoughtful when utilizing that tool.

4. **Keep the end goal in mind.** As a teacher, your goal during any situation involving misbehavior should be for that misbehavior to never occur again. When you provide a consequence to a student, it is critically important for you to always remember that end goal. Although in the moment you may be frustrated or mad, there is most likely a reason that student misbehaved. It could have been caused by boredom, frustration with the task, or even a misunderstanding about cultural norms. No matter what the cause is, you must work to figure it out and address it because no matter what occurred, you do not want it to happen again. If that student was bored, consider adapting your lessons to the interest of your students. If that student was frustrated with the task, teach him or her healthy ways to deal with frustration and persevere. If that student was acting in a way that would be appropriate at home but not at school, let him or her know that you understand their background, but reiterate that even if that behavior is accepted at home, it is not at school. In each of these situations, it is important to implement your consequence so you are consistent with your expectations, but you must never forget that your goal is for that misbehavior to not occur again.

Once the school year starts, you will most likely tweak what you implement, or maybe even entirely overhaul it! This will be discussed in depth later in chapter 14. What is important is that you have a system in place that you have thought through before the students walk in, so you are ready to handle misbehavior right when the bell rings first day of school.

When brainstorming ideas on what to use, I would highly recommend observing teachers, reading classroom management books and articles, talking to mentors, and even browsing teacher blogs. Many people (even researchers!) have differing ideas on what management strategies work, thus you must use your best judgment to sift through all of the information you will find to discover the best fit for you and your classroom. Remember— positive reinforcement is going to be the heart of your management strategy, but you will also have a consequence "tool belt" you can use when it is necessary.

Also, do not forget that the school you will first work for may (hopefully!) have a detailed school behavior system. Now, not all schools are able to use these effectively, but they do generally help in moments of major crisis, such as physical violence. So when considering your consequence plan, remember that if behavior escalates to where physical safety issues are occurring (i.e., students bursting into a heated argument, student running out of the classroom, etc.), it is most likely best to contact administration to help you handle that situation.

Below are three examples of how beginning year teachers decided their management system.

Ms. Taylor was a first year kindergarten teacher in a high-poverty school. She wanted to be as prepared as possible for her first day of school, so she researched a variety of different classroom management systems online. After looking through a multitude of them, she decided on one that she found on a teaching blog. This teacher used a tally system to reward her students. Each student had his or her own tally chart, and students could rack up tallies any time they were being "superstars," yet they would lose a tally when they needed a consequence for bad behavior. Once a student earned a certain number of tallies, they could "cash them in" for special rewards, like extra reading time or trading chairs with the teacher for the day. Ms. Taylor chose this management strategy because it seemed clean and simple, and she did not want to choose something too complex going into her first year. She also liked it because she knew that if she worked at it, she could make sure to give many more tallies than take them away. This way, it could help build her positive classroom culture while also giving her something she could rely on if a student misbehaved.

Mr. Nelson was a first year middle school special education teacher. His position was going to look different than many other teachers because he was going to be teaching a small group of special education students in a classroom that also had mainstream students. Even with these extra challenges, he knew that he wanted to have his own small-scale system that he could rely on in a time of need. He knew that the school policy was to send students to the "take-a-break" seat if they were having trouble being successful, thus he felt confident that could be a good consequence for when students misbehaved. He then thought through what his positive reinforcement would be because he knew that was the most important part of his teaching! Since he was told that his particular students would need more reinforcement than most, he decided on giving students one point at the end of each lesson. Mr. Nelson would keep track of these points on his tablet, and once a student reached 10 points they could have lunch with him some time that week. Mr. Nelson really felt comfortable with this strategy because he knew that since the consequence was something that the classroom teachers implemented as well, he would be consistent with their expectations while also being able to focus on positive reinforcement.

Mrs. Wilson was a first year high school music teacher. When thinking about what management strategy she wanted to use, she thought she would want to focus on students taking care of their school instruments. She was going to plan some type of "bring your own device" day at the end of each quarter for students who never damaged an instrument. After talking to a colleague and reading a classroom management book, however, she realized a few flaws in her thinking. First, what if a really great student accidentally damaged an instrument in the second week of school? Would she really want that moment to define the rest of the quarter for that student? Mrs. Wilson also realized that focusing on more frequent, and non-tangible rewards would coincide more with her beliefs and understandings of student motivation. Thus, she made a list of different ways that she could positively reinforce students verbally. That way, students were getting "rewards" every single day! She also decided that her consequences for misbehavior would be a general flowchart that she had borrowed from a mentor teacher. First, a student would get a warning (and she would mark the warning on the attendance sheet). Then, the student would be asked to sit out of the activity until he or she was ready to return. Finally, if the misbehavior continued, she would follow school protocol and send the student to a buddy room.

Stay Focused on the Real Goal

Keep in mind that no reward in a classroom will really ever have a high level tangible value. You are not going to give away the latest technology device at the end of each week in a raffle. Your real goal should be to have personal positive feedback from the teacher as a high-desired outcome. An eventual aim is to have a smile, a friendly nod from the teacher, or the teacher saying a phrase like, "Wow, you are working so hard!" be the ultimate reinforcement. Ms. Taylor, Mr. Nelson, and Mrs. Wilson's management strategies will not be effective without regular, informal, positive interactions with students. As discussed previously, having positive relationships with your students is the foundation of a well-managed classroom, and these regular, informal, and positive interactions will allow you to consistently develop the culture you desire.

Having positive relationships with your students is the foundation of a well-managed classroom.

Lesson Planning and Instruction

Lesson Planning: Down to the Minute

A key thing that helps new teachers succeed occurs when the students are not in the classroom: lesson planning. During your undergraduate career, you may have had classes that taught you how to write an extensive lesson plan, requiring you to think through your objective, the materials you need, how you will introduce the topic, etc. Although those may have been helpful when thinking through how to teach effectively, they may not be helpful when planning for the first few weeks of school. During these crucial days, you will be figuring out how to be a teacher. You honestly may not care about what the objective is for your lesson—you just want to survive the day. College professors are great for helping you plan a lesson focused on academic instruction, but this section will help you plan your day as a first year teacher who is still figuring out how to manage students, let alone teach them the alphabet or calculus.

Even though you may not feel like you know what you are doing during these first days, it is critically important to *look* like you know what you are doing. That does not mean suddenly becoming a "know-it-all" even if you make a mistake; it means to have something for students to be doing at every moment of every block, period, or lesson. For example, maybe the teacher asks students to complete an assignment, but three students finish it in two minutes and have nothing to do once they are done. That time after they have completed their assignment is "down time," and for new teachers it can potentially cause significant issues for both students and teachers. According to Todd Whitaker's research on teaching quality (2012), very little occurs at random in an effective teacher's classroom because they always have a "plan and purpose for everything they do" (p. 79). Fortunately, even as a first year teacher you can attain this same quality by avoiding "down time," or time where one or many students have nothing to do.

Even though you may not feel like you know what you are doing during these first days, it is critically important to *look* like you know what you are doing.

Down time is dangerous for two reasons. First, it is a waste of precious instructional time. Many educators agree that there are not enough hours in the day to teach students everything they need. Thus, every single minute should be planned for because even five wasted minutes each day of school leads to hours of lost instructional time over a school year. If you are teaching a 1st grader how to read, or an 8th grader how to derive the slope of a line, those lost minutes could directly lead to decreased understanding of the material. The second reason that down time is dangerous is because it causes a break in structure. As educators, we know that the most effectively run classrooms are ones with tight structures that help students succeed. Well, if you are teaching a lesson, but somehow you planned it to where only three quarters of the class is participating, what are the other students doing? As mentioned before, some will simply lose focus, which may not be a huge detriment to you, but it could cause students to lose precious learning opportunities. Others, however, may use that "down time" to distract classmates, check their social media feeds, or even disrupt the teacher. And once one student has lost focus in one way or another, the likelihood of others joining in is high.

To prevent such issues, you must *overplan* during the first few weeks of school. Yes, we said overplan! You never want to end up being a teacher who went through his or her entire lesson, and now has a class of 28 students with eight minutes of "down time" before the bell rings. During moments like those, even the best-behaving students will have trouble sitting quietly. When you are planning, map out what your day looks like down to the minute. Think through what students will do when they first walk into your classroom, what they will do when they complete their assignment, what they will do when only five of the students in the class are volunteering to write answers on the board, etc. You must prevent "down time" as much as possible. Additionally, always be prepared for students who finish early. Whatever you decide to have them do, make sure that it is something that enriches their learning instead of extra busy work that punishes them for being expedient.

Now, some of you may have principals or teams who require you to write and turn in lesson plans that are this detailed. If that is the case, you can use those as your guides when preventing "down time." If you do not have this requirement, however, we have included two real-life examples of how first year teachers planned the first day of school. Although one is for an elementary teacher and one is for a secondary teacher, notice the similarities. They both have extensive and detailed plans down to the minute for what the first day looks like.

Elementary Example

8:00–8:20 Morning work. I hand students morning work at the door. Remind them of what the morning expectations are (voices off, put all materials in lockers, eat breakfast in their seat). They put morning work face-down on their desk when they are finished. They can then read or write until announcements.

8:20–8:40 Morning meeting. I explain to students how they should transition to the carpet after announcements (quietly, calmly, and find a successful spot in the circle). During the meeting, I introduce hand signals to students (posted on the board), and explain bathroom expectations (two passes: one for morning and one for afternoon). Then I explain what our class promise is and we brainstorm what this looks like in different scenarios (classroom, lunchroom, recess, etc.).

8:40–8:50 Count around the circle. Students count around the circle by ones. I ask a volunteer to begin the circle, and that student decides the direction to go around. First circle, start at zero. Next one, start at 47. Next one, count down from 85.

8:50–9:00 Math carpet spots. I assign students their carpet spots and have them practice coming from their circle spot to the carpet spot. I explain why we have assigned spots (to make sure we are all successful), and then have them practice the transition from circle to carpet a few times until they show success.

9:00–9:15 What do mathematicians do? I explain that in our classroom, all students are mathematicians. Talk about what a mathematician is, and then we brainstorm as a class what mathematicians do. I have them share their ideas with a shoulder partner before they share with the class. Write down ideas on the pre-prepared anchor chart.

9:15–9:40 Mathematicians art project. I explain to students the artwork they will create using the anchor chart we created together. Explain how students should get their materials, and then have them practice it. Before they begin, I remind them that they can talk to their table-mates but it must not be a "loud and proud" voice level. Maybe have them practice talking at that voice level if necessary.

9:40–9:50 Practice lining up. Tell students what their line order is, and have them practice getting in line a few times. Challenge them to do it as quietly and calmly as possible. Also, I explain that we will now be going to the gym, and we practice (in the classroom) what it looks like to walk to the gym in an appropriate manner.

9:50–10:10 School-wide rally in the gym. (Our class seating location is the front right corner.)

10:10–10:20 Introduce writer's workshop. I explain that one of the things we will do each day is write. We brainstorm as a class why we write (helps brains grow, helps us become better writers and readers, helps with spelling, handwriting, etc.), and I write down ideas on anchor chart. We then brainstorm what it looks like to do independent writings (voices off, eyes on paper, pencils moving, etc.), and I write down those ideas too.

10:20–10:30 Teach three independent writing activities. I explain and model three of the "you choose" writing activities they will be able to do (recipe, list, poem). Give examples of each writing choice, and take student examples as well. Students whisper in their fists which choice they are making today, hand out the papers, and students head to their seat to begin writing.

10:30–10:40 Practice writing activities. Students practice writing, and I walk around helping students stay on task, come up with ideas, and compliment them on hard work and creativity. Around 10:38, I share a few things that I saw them do that "good writers" do.

10:40–10:55 First day read aloud. Students practice coming to their carpet spot, and once they do it well, I then read the book.

10:55–11:00 Walk to music. Students practice lining up again and we head to music.

Hour-Long High School Algebra II Class

Passing Period. As students are arriving to class, I remind them to read the board so they are ready for class when the bell rings. On the board I have a list of four things they need to be successful for the day.

Am I ready for class?

1. Homework from last night out and on my desk
2. Pencil
3. Calculator
4. Whiteboard supplies (personal whiteboard, expo marker, eraser)

10:00–10:10. I walk in, thank students for being ready and put a warm-up problem up on the board. They are to try it on their own, compare answers with the people around them, then I will randomly select someone to put all of their work up on the front board for us to discuss. As students are working on this problem, I am walking around the room with a clipboard taking completion grades on their homework. I use this time to discuss homework completion with students individually and also give hints as they work on the warm-up problem.

10:10–10:15. Use the "random student selector" button I have through our attendance program and have that student go up and work through the warm-up problem. He or she talks through solving the problem then other students share other ways they solved it. Ask students to put their whiteboard supplies aside and place their homework in front of them.

10:15–10:25. Project the answer key to their homework onto the screen at the front of the classroom. I read five answers aloud then pause to take questions over those five problems. Continue this process until we have discussed all the answers. Talking through any of their questions, working problems on the board for them, or walking around helping them find and correct any errors they made.

10:25–10:40. Pass out a notesheet and we begin our lesson on simplifying rational expressions. I do five examples for the class that increase in difficulty each time. Pause frequently, asking students what their gut tells them to do next and why. Note-taking is more of a discussion than a lecture.

10:40–10:45. Put a final problem on the board and ask them to try it on their own using the whiteboard supplies from earlier. As students finish, I check their work. If they are correct I compliment them, ask them to put their whiteboard supplies away, and give them a worksheet to work on for the remainder of the hour. If they are incorrect, we discover their mistake together and work to correct things until they reach the answer.

10:45–10:55. Once everyone has the worksheet, I circulate around the classroom checking in with students and answer questions.

10:55–11:00. I put the answers to the first three problems on the board and ask students to check and make sure they were able to get there. If they were not, I ask them to speak up now so we can work together to find the answer.

11:00. The bell rings and I tell them all to have an amazing rest of their day as they exit my room.

Instruction: Focus on Engagement

The reason that we only focused a minimal amount of time on *what* you should be teaching is because that is something that will change a lot. Curriculum is regularly modified and even overhauled based on initiatives, leadership changes, and even political climate. Thus, instead of focusing on *what* you are going to teach during your first year, focus on *how* you are going to teach it. Although there are a variety of effective teaching strategies that we know you will come across and utilize as you grow throughout your career, we are only going to focus on student engagement in this book. Student engagement can be defined as "Students' psychological investment in and effort directed toward learning, understanding, or mastering the knowledge, skills, or crafts that academic work is intended to promote" (Newmann, Wehlage, & Lamborn, 1992, p. 12). Research has found there to be much potential in classrooms with high student engagement, with the benefits summarized nicely by Fredricks, Blumenfeld, and Paris: "Ultimately, although engagement might begin with liking or participating, it can result in commitment or investment and thus may be a key to diminishing student apathy and enhanced learning" (2004, p. 82).

Imagine two history classes taught by two different teachers: Ms. Summers and Ms. Jackson. Both are first year teachers. They instruct in the same school, work with the same clientele, and teach the same subject matter. When you walk into Ms. Summers' class, most of the time students passively sit in their desks day after day copying down notes that the teacher has written on the board. After that, they read the textbook and then listen to the teacher lecture about what they read. During the silent reading time, Ms. Summers regularly has behavior issues with students texting, passing notes, and sometimes even cracking jokes at her expense. She is frustrated that the students will not do what she asks of them, and is starting to forget why she went into teaching in the first place. She may even cynically think to herself, "Kids nowadays just don't want to learn."

Just down the hallway, in Ms. Jackson's classroom, a different situation can be seen. Although students do have to copy down notes and listen to lecture, they only do this for 15 minutes of the class. During the rest of the period, they spend time walking around the room to compare and contrast historical events on large chart paper posted on the walls, partner-read the textbook to find key details about that day's topic, and use technology to find recent culturally relevant articles that connect to their learning objectives for the day. Although Ms. Jackson definitely does not feel like her year is going perfectly, she is pleased overall because she has had minimal behavior issues, and students seem to be engaged in her lessons most of the time. The first year of teaching has definitely taken a lot of work, but she is pleased to dedicate extra time to her lessons because she can tell that good things are coming from them.

As you can see in the examples, there are many things that Ms. Summers and Ms. Jackson are doing differently. For the purpose of this section, however, we want you to focus on the engagement strategies they are using. In Ms. Summers' classroom, she is teaching in ways that do not have students actively engaged in the material. She is having students passively take notes, read silently, and listen to lecture. Ms. Jackson, on the other hand, is getting students moving around, giving them opportunities to interact with peers, and integrate culturally relevant pedagogy into the materials.

Although we used Ms. Jackson's classroom as an example, do not think that this is what your room must look like every day. How you will make your lessons engaging all depends on your students, your grade-level, your subject matter, the development of your management abilities, etc. Also remember that the purpose of these examples is *not* to say that note-taking, lecture, and silent reading never have a place in the classroom. Many times students *do* need to take notes so they have material to study, and you will need to provide direct instruction about new content. Thus, instead of debating about whether or not those instructional strategies have a place in the classroom, we want you to always simply ask yourself, "How engaged will my students be throughout the lesson I am going to teach today?"

Making this a focus of your instruction on a daily basis provides a two-fold benefit. First, it prevents behavior issues. If students are interested in your lessons, they will be less likely to do something disruptive. Ms. Summers was teaching in a way that led students to be bored. When bored, students who already struggle in school will be tempted to disrupt the classroom because they will find something that keeps their attention better (which is something that we would all consider doing!). In Ms. Jackson's classroom, however, most students were too busy to even think about anything other than what they are learning. When you have students actively engaged in the material, there won't be enough time for them to text their friends. Second, research has found that student engagement is strongly connected to academic achievement (Marks, 2000). If students are interested in your lessons, they are much more likely to learn whatever you are teaching. This is huge, because obviously as a teacher, it is your job to educate your students!

Now, it simply comes down to the *how* of creating engaging lessons. Developing your teaching craft is a goal that will be ever-evolving. You may have seen experienced teachers down the hall who seem to have all their students sitting at the edge of their seats every day and may have thought, "There is no way I will be able to do that during my first year!" Please do not compare yourself to the highly effective, veteran teachers you have observed, because their knowledge of instructional strategies has developed over many years of experience.

Instead, when you are planning, think, "What is *one* way I can engage my students in a meaningful way during this lesson?" Notice how we only said to try *one* at first. We did this because when you are teaching during your first year, you are just beginning to learn how to instruct effectively—and that is a large feat to figure out! Thus, feel free to start small. For example, if you are a first grade teacher and you are teaching the reading strategy "stretch the word out," teach them a hand motion that goes with that strategy and have them practice it when reading a tough word. If you are a 7th grade geometry teacher, have students use individual whiteboards when answering questions instead of having them raise their hands, so every single student is answering each question, instead of just one. If you are a high school music teacher, use culturally relevant music that students enjoy or relate to to teach rhythms or chord progressions.

As you continue to grow as a teacher over your first few weeks and months, you will progress to more advanced teaching strategies. When this occurs, you will be able to focus more on engagement *along with* effective instructional strategies. Luckily, your instruction will actually be improved because you focused so heavily on engagement from day 1! For "future you," there are many resources available that will help build your repertoire of instructional techniques, including other faculty at your school, instructional coaches, administration, Twitter, blogs, websites, and publications.

But What About Curriculum?

When it comes to curriculum, every school and district is different. Some schools will require you to adhere to a set curriculum with minimal "wiggle-room." Other schools may have a curriculum there for you to use, but they are flexible with how you implement it. Finally, there are some schools that have no curriculum to use at all, thus you and your team will be in charge of figuring out the best way to meet the mandatory standards. No matter what situation you find yourself in, focus on simplicity.

These curricula could be very strong or not-so-great, and either way, if you have them, *use them*. Not only use them because you will most likely be legally obligated to, but because they will help make your life simpler as you navigate your way through the first few weeks and months of school. You are going to be overwhelmed with myriad tasks and obstacles at the beginning of the year, so when you are first planning lessons, do not be afraid to use whatever materials are provided for you, or find "pre-made" materials that apply to the standard you are teaching. As you develop your knowledge of standards and curriculum, you will develop a more critical eye of the content you are teaching your students. This is something that great master-teachers do instinctually, but as a beginning teacher, be patient with yourself. It is not your job (yet) to write the most creative lesson plans on the planet—this is when you use the expertise of others to help you stay afloat, whether those "others" are your teammates, curriculum writers in your district, or publishing companies.

Instead of focusing on the curriculum you are teaching, make it a priority to believe that your students can achieve at high levels. Push yourself to avoid "dumbing down" content because you don't think your students can handle it, or because a member of your team said that your kids just are not smart enough. Instead, focus on scaffolding the material, or providing necessary supports, in ways that help them achieve. There

> **Instead of focusing on the curriculum you are teaching, make it a priority to believe that your students can achieve at high levels.**

is a chance that you are the only person in your students' lives who truly believes that they can achieve at high levels, so do not let yourself be the hindrance to pushing your students to greatness.

Section II

The Students Are Here ... Now What?

Explaining and Practicing Procedures

Half of what makes procedures effective is the teacher thoroughly thinking them through, and then preparing the classroom for them. The other half, however, is what the teacher does once the students are at school. This is where the application of the procedures comes in—and the teacher's clear teaching and consistent reinforcement of them is critical. Let's imagine the first day of school. You see your first student walking down the hallway, and you are prepared to greet her at the door. The first two procedures you will need to address are how she should enter your classroom, and what she should do after she enters. Starting from the moment she steps up to the door, begin to set her up for what your expectations will be.

Here is what an effective first interaction with an elementary student could look like. (All of this is said with a confident smile—remember *you* are the teacher.) "Good morning! My name is Ms. Whitaker, and I am going to be your teacher for this year. I am very excited to meet you! This morning, I will be looking for two things: One is for you to put your backpack in your locker, and the second is for you to find the seat with your name on it and begin your morning work without any talking. Can you repeat what my two expectations will be for this morning, and every morning?" (Student repeats the two expectations.) "Great! I can tell that you are going to be an outstanding student this year!"

Here is what an effective first interaction with a secondary student could be. (As with the previous example, this is yet again said with a confident smile.) "Good morning! My name is Ms. Whitaker and I am going to be your algebra teacher for this semester. Please go find a seat and start quietly filling out the beginning-of-the-year survey I have on each desk."

Although these are two different examples, we want you to notice the similarities between them. In both situations, Ms. Whitaker is letting students know two things: what is expected of them before they even enter the classroom, and what the classroom climate is. With the smile paired with the clear and firm expectations, she has now shown her students that she will be caring, yet structured. Kearney and McCroskey (1980) found that "students who perceived teachers as decisive, deliberate, challenging, and dynamic also reported greater affect and behavioral commitment toward the teacher, class, and subject content" (p. 547). Thus, although you do want to prioritize seeming welcoming and warm when you first meet students, you also must equally prioritize exuding confidence when laying out expectations during the first minutes, hours, and days of your year.

Students are extremely intuitive, and your first impression will be critical to the dynamic of the first days and weeks of school.

Students are extremely intuitive, and your first impression will be critical to the dynamic of the first days and weeks of school.

Even though we have given you two examples, you will need to adjust them to fit your setting. Sometimes you could end up with a fairly independent class of 5th graders that doesn't need to repeat your expectations every time they enter, or you may have a class of 12th graders that could benefit from that type of regular reminder. Either way, it is important to err on the side of caution and be as explicit as possible with your expectations. As stated earlier, it is much easier to loosen up procedures as the year goes on than it is to tighten them.

As you work through your first days and weeks, you will need to explain (and possibly re-explain) your procedures for each activity you do. Whether you are teaching 1st grade or 11th grade, you must let your students know how to complete whatever task you are asking them to do. Remember: It is always easier to start out with tight structures and get more lax than to do the reverse. Thus, when introducing any structures in your classroom, follow these steps:

1. Explain the task you want students to complete
2. Model how you want it completed
3. Have a few students model or explain how you want it completed
4. Have the task completed in small groups (may be skipped depending on the task and the students' level of independence)
5. Have the task completed as a whole class (after success)

* If students are not successful with one step, repeat that step until you find success.

Notice how we started out being extremely explicit with what we expected, through our words and actions. Once we felt like we had explained it well enough, we then had one or two students model it themselves. We do this to make sure that students are understanding what we are asking, while also giving the students not modeling a chance to see it done well again. As students are modeling, we point out the things that students are doing that we like. If a student does something incorrectly, we ask the student to do it again after explaining the correction in a gentle manner. For example, "I love how Jennie quietly walked over to her locker. Jennie, can I actually have you do it one more time walking the other way around the room? I think that may help with traffic flow when pack-up time is actually going on." We did not criticize what Jennie did, but we did have her do it again while explaining why and emphasizing that is how we want it done from now on. After that, we had students complete it in small groups, and then if students have done it successfully in small groups for a few days, we could then have the entire class do it at the same time (although this should only be used when you feel confident that your whole class can be successful in this looser structure).

You may feel like your students are too old to do steps such as modeling, pointing out what others are doing well, etc. Many secondary teachers incorrectly assume the students know what to do. A challenge is if they do not know the correct way, it becomes difficult to build the relationships you desire because you now have to correct students instead of reinforcing them doing the desired procedures. You can trust your instincts on this but remember that it is much more challenging to tighten structures and expectations than it is to loosen them. Following are an elementary and secondary example of how to teach and practice procedures. When reading these, pay attention to how the teachers use explanation, examples, and language to help their students correctly implement procedures.

In Mr. Smith's 2nd grade classroom, students are learning how to appropriately line up in line order. He had the line order posted on the board, and he explained the task he needed his students to complete clearly. "Class, right now, since we are about to head to lunch, we are going to practice lining up at the door. When we line up, we calmly stand out of our seats, push our chairs in, and quietly walk to our line spot. I am going to show you how to do it." Mr. Smith models it, and then asks students to point out things that he did that made it a successful transition. After this, he continues, "Now that you have seen what it looks like to line up in my classroom, can I have a volunteer model this for everyone? Thank you for raising your hand, Devonte. Can you show the class how a 2nd grader should line up?" While Devonte is modeling this, Mr. Smith points out all of the things that he likes that Devonte is doing. "Wow, notice how Devonte considerately pushed in his chair, and calmly walked to the line. Also, he was so quiet I don't think I heard his shoes tap the ground!" After Devonte returns to his seat, Mr. Smith asks for another volunteer, and this time he asks the *students* to point out things that the new student is doing well while transitioning. Finally, Mr. Smith wants to release the students in table groups, but before he does, this is how he sets up his students for success: "Now that I see what incredible students I have in my class, I can tell we are ready to get lined up for lunch! Don't forget—I am looking for students who calmly stand out of your seat, push your chair in, and quietly line up. Which table group thinks they can do this the best?" Mr. Smith will then dismiss each table group until everyone is lined up.

This example is perfect for young students who need extremely tight structures and explanations. What about older students, or ones who may not need such repetition, and who may have more extensive instructions to follow? In Ms. Logan's 8th grade social studies class, she is teaching students how they will need to grade and turn in their bellringer each day. "Every day you will come into class with a bellringer, or a task to do right when you enter the classroom, on the board. You will have five minutes to complete it." As Ms. Logan continues to explain the procedure, she is walking around and modeling each step. While doing this, she refers to the list of steps she has displayed on the board. "If you complete the bellringer before the five-minute timer goes off, I will want you to check one of the answer sheets I will have face down on the table in the front of the room. If you get it correct, you can turn your bellringer in to the homework bin, and if you get it incorrect you can head back to your seat and explain why you had the misconception that you did on your paper with a pen. When you have turned it in, you can sit quietly at your seat and read or write. Once the five-minute timer goes off, I will then collect all of the papers."

Ms. Logan realizes that she shared a lot of steps in that explanation, so she knows it is crucial to ask students to reiterate what she had just explained. "Can someone tell me in their own words what you do if you finish before the five-minute timer goes off?" If students can successfully explain this, she can continue to ask about each of the different steps. If students cannot, then she will re-explain and model the steps again herself before asking them to explain it again. Before she has a student model the procedure, she reiterates her high expectations. "Class, I have one final, critically important part of our procedure: It must be silent the entire time because most of our bellringers will be independent work, and I want everyone to be able to concentrate as much as possible without distraction." Now she knows that the class is ready for a faux bellringer practice session. First, she has one or two students model what it looks like to check their work and then return to their seat. She decides to skip the fourth step of having the task completed using small groups because she feels comfortable with the level of independence her students have shown.

During the whole-class practice session, Ms. Logan is walking around, quietly pointing out things that students are doing well, while also redirecting students who have forgotten the steps. "Sarah, you grade in purple pen!? That's awesome, I wish I had one." "Jacoby, your handwriting is better than mine. Thank you for making your work so neat and organized." "Tyler, you got done so quickly. I appreciate your hard work. What book are you reading? Is it good?" Notice how Ms. Logan is reinforcing the behavior she is looking for, but in a more discreet way. Instead of saying outright, "Sarah, thank you for grading your paper in pen," Ms. Logan makes a comment that aims at building a relationship while still emphasizing the behavior she is looking for. In this type of interaction, she uses her knowledge about the type of feedback her students best respond to, and then applies it directly to the situation.

After the five-minute timer goes off and she has collected the bellringers, she then has students give feedback as to what went well and what could improve for next time. The feedback could be what went well as a whole class or what the specific student liked about the activity. "Everyone in the room was so quiet!" "I liked that I could rework and make corrections to my problem in pen." The changes to make next time better could also be about what the whole class could fix or an individual student. "Do you think it would be better if we all took the same path up to the answer key so people do not bump into each other?" "I need to not forget to bring a reading book to class!" Although some of the students were successful with this bellringer, there were a few who were not. Thus, Ms. Logan decides to try it again with a different problem to make sure that every student knows exactly what is expected. "All of your feedback was right on target. I have another great brain-busting question ready so we can practice this procedure one more time. I want this to be streamlined so we are ready for the real thing tomorrow!"

8

Managing Your Classroom

Managing Yourself

Before we even begin to discuss how to manage your students, we want you to know that the number one rule for handling any and every behavior situation is managing yourself. You will notice that in almost every scenario, we will describe how you should be "calm," "firm" or "confident." You can never control every single thing a child does, but you can control every single thing that *you* do. Tom and Marsha Savage from Santa Clara University argue why teachers

> **The number one rule for handling any and every behavior situation is managing yourself.**

must "respect the dignity of the student" in their book *Successful Classroom Management and Discipline: Teaching Self Control and Responsibility* (2009, p. 131). They say that teachers must "respect the dignity of the student" for two reasons: We have a moral obligation to do so, and it will help prevent students from "striking back" since they will not feel the need to go on the defensive. The way that you as a new teacher can prioritize doing this is by managing yourself.

Thus, when you are reading through the different behavior management situations and techniques, always remember that what you do and how you handle it is what will decide if the situation goes well or goes poorly. Though you have a great deal of influence on affecting student behavior, you have 100 percent influence on your own behavior. Thus that should always be the starting point. Use this section to reflect on your previously held conceptions about student management and behavior, and be prepared to either reinforce or re-evaluate your beliefs about how to manage students. Just remember that it always starts with *you*.

In addition, please never forget that you are the adult in the situation, and thus you must hold yourself to such standards. Adults should not argue, ridicule, or demean when managing behavior. Also, adults should not hold grudges. Just as we hope people forgive us if we make mistakes, students want the same thing. If a student has a bad "moment," you handle the moment in an appropriate way, but then move on. Moving on may take one minute if the behavior is minor, or it may take two hours if it was a more significant incident. Either way, always remember that every day is a new day, and students need to feel welcome in your class no matter what happened the day before. You are the adult, and you must be the model. So, no arguing, no ridiculing, no demeaning language, and especially, no holding grudges.

Before we begin, it is important to remember that although there are a multitude of behavior management techniques that will be discussed, there is no "silver bullet" in managing a classroom. What this chapter should do is fill your bag with a large handful of behavior management "tricks." You must always remember that one type of response will never work with each student in every situation. Instead, our hope is that this gives you a solid starting point as you begin your teaching journey. Then, throughout your first year, and the years to come, you will add plenty more "tricks" from experience, research, and colleagues. Now let's look at a few different strategies you can use to manage your first classroom.

Subtle Steering

Picture this: You have gotten about half of your class into their seats, quietly doing their first task, when you notice your student

Kathleen has begun to talk to her classmate Akio. You know that the student knows your expectations since you had each one repeat them to you before they entered the classroom. This is your first behavior management moment. What do you do?

The most important thing to remember is that your first instinct should never be to scold or point out what negative action is occurring. Instead, you should always want to de-escalate the situation; keep as few students involved as possible. Great teachers shrink issues instead of inflating them, and there are many ways to do this. When you notice Kathleen talking, the first thing you can do is use proximity. Instead of making the problem larger and bringing other students into the situation by saying, "Kathleen, you know better than to talk right now!" simply walk over toward her. If she notices you are hovering, nine times out of ten she will remember what your expectations were and zip her lips right then and there. If she does not notice, then gently tap her on the back to let her know that you know what is occurring.

Your day continues on, and proximity is generally working for you. What if there is a time that it does not? What is the next least-invasive form of management? As a teacher, your goal should be to keep your classroom climate positive, thus another way to "subtly steer" student misbehavior is pointing out positive behaviors you see. This is greatly beneficial because it builds a warm classroom climate, handles student misbehavior, and informs other students of what behaviors you appreciate seeing. For example, let's pretend you are a 1st grade teacher, and it is silent reading time in your classroom. You notice your student Nara dazing off into space. It would be ineffective to say, "Nara, get back on task!" Instead, you could walk up to Nara and say, "Wow, Nara, I love how you are holding that book so appropriately. I cannot wait to hear what you think about it!" Since Nara knows that it is silent reading time, this comment will build her up while also gently reminding her that she should be reading. Now let's pretend you are an 8th grade P.E. teacher. You have asked three students to collect the basketballs at the end of class, but one of them has decided to shoot around instead of picking up the basketballs. Instead of yelling at that student to stop messing around, you could instead say to one of the others, "Hey, thanks for picking these up quickly. You know what a stickler I am about quick clean-up!" By giving that compliment, you reminded the other student to pick up quickly without creating a scene and negatively affecting the classroom climate.

An important part of this positive reinforcement is remembering that your comments must be *genuine*. You cannot thank students for doing what you asked with the motivation of getting them to repeat the action. Kids are intuitive, and just like adults, they do not like to be thanked by someone with an ulterior motive. This all ties back to a teacher's authentic love of their job. If you truly care about the students sitting in front of you, you *will* be genuine when you thank them. You realize that going to school is hard work, and since you have such high expectations as a teacher, you truly appreciate when they follow directions. It is also important to remember that positive reinforcement is a critical aspect of building rapport with students, as noted previously, and the better relationship you have with a student, the more effective this strategy will be.

As you continue to master proximity and positive comments, many of you will still have behavior to manage. Thus, let us pretend that you are teaching a whole-class lesson, and one of your students, Aiden, is "messing around" with materials in the back of the room. You use your proximity strategy, tap him on the back, and thank classmates near him for listening respectfully, but none of those has worked. A different response you could make is take the materials out of his hands and as genuinely as you possibly can, say, "I can put those away for you." Notice you must say this as genuinely as you possibly can. As frustrated as you may feel in this moment, you must make the student feel like you are truly wanting to help him out, not punishing him for "messing around." Also notice that the teacher did not say, "Give those to me," and then wait for him to hand over the materials. Instead, the teacher took the materials out of Aiden's hand almost exactly as the statement was being said. This helps solve the problem without creating a power-struggle or making a scene that involves the rest of the class.

A final subtle-steering technique is including the struggling student in the lesson more. For example, you could call on him to answer a question, ask him to help you write information on the board, or even do a quick 30-second partner share and listen in on his conversation to hold him accountable. As mentioned previously, lesson planning is another form of behavior management, and the more entertaining and effective your lesson structure is, the fewer behavior problems you will have.

With a student like this, or in any of the previous scenarios we have used, if necessary, we may also take a minute or two to talk to the student outside of the classroom, or during a passing period or break, just to check up and see if anything else was going on. You could say something like, "Aiden, I noticed that you did not seem like yourself today. Is everything okay?" This conversation helps Aiden know that you did notice his misbehavior, but you are also genuinely concerned about his well-being. These quick conversations can be extremely critical when building relationships with your most struggling students. There is a chance that Aiden was still mad about something that happened at home that morning, or maybe he had extra energy that day. No matter what comes from this dialogue, you always want to go into it with genuine concern for the student. Assuming that the student did not behave with malicious intent gives you the freedom to use these quick conversations to build strong relationships.

Direct Redirection

The next option that you have for managing student behavior is called "direct redirection." It is called this because instead of avoiding directly addressing the issues, you now face them head on in calm and confident ways. Let us go back to the first example provided: You have a student named Kathleen, and she is very chatty during a lesson. You tried proximity; it didn't work. You complimented those around her; it didn't work. You even engaged her in the lesson more; it still didn't work! It is now time to be more direct with her because she either has not gotten the hint, or is knowingly defying what your expectations are.

The first thing you can do is to walk over to Kathleen and have a quiet, serious, but quick conversation. It is time for her to stop distracting her classmates because you know that instructional time is critically important, and she is starting to affect the learning of her classmates and your ability to focus on your teaching. There are two ways that you can hold this conversation, depending on how severe the situation is. In both situations, you are never mean, demeaning, or sarcastic. You are simply firm. In the first scenario, you begin by explaining that you "get" why the student is doing what she is doing, but then explain why it needs to stop. For example, you could whisper, "Kathleen, I totally understand that right now algebra is not as exciting as talking with your classmates. However, I take instructional time seriously and I need you to also take it seriously because I care about you and your learning. It's time to stay focused so you can be successful." When you said this to Kathleen, you were not mean, but you were firm so she knew you meant everything that you said: that you understood why she was disengaged, that you meant that you cared about her, and that you meant that she must pay attention to succeed.

Another way to have this private conversation is to simply to tell her how you are feeling, what she is doing to cause it, and tell her what she needs to do instead, all with a firm tone. As opposed to the previous example, this can be used when the behavior was more disruptive, or when you may honestly have feelings that were hurt. For example, you could whisper, "Kathleen, I do not appreciate how you are distracting your classmates while I am teaching. I need you to sit back in your seat and stay focused on my lesson so you stop distracting yourself and those around you." Instead of empathizing with the student as we did in the previous example, you are letting her know who her behaviour is affecting and that it needs to stop. One thing that is similar with both examples though is that you explained *why* you need the behavior to stop. This is critically important because it gives more of an opportunity for the student to buy in to your request, which prevents power struggles that can be detrimental to a classroom climate and teacher–student relationship.

Let's say that you are in a situation that does not allow you to walk across the room to a student who is misbehaving. You may be a 3rd grade teacher teaching a guided reading lesson, or a 9th grade teacher having a one-on-one writing conference with a student. Either way, it will waste serious instructional time if you have to interrupt your lesson, get out of your chair, and walk across the room to reprimand a student. Although some researchers argue that you should never do a public reprimand of a student, sometimes the realities of the teaching profession do not always allow teachers to work in a "best case" scenario. So we must work with the best tools that we have within the situations we are in. Thus, we will explain how to do public redirections that address student misbehavior in an appropriate way.

The first thing you can do is to make eye contact with the student, Jordan, from across the room if possible. Depending on the way he is misbehaving, the next step you take could go in two different directions. If he is doing something minor like accidentally tapping his pencil loudly, or leaning over to whisper to a friend, you can pair the eye contact with a silent friendly warning, like a signal for him to be quiet, or you mouthing with a smile "Please stop … thank you!" If he is doing something more serious, and you have already given him a friendly warning to quit his behavior, you can give him a more serious look. For example, you could raise your eyebrows or purse your lips just enough for him to know that what he is doing is wrong, and that it must stop. Both of these strategies are entirely quiet but direct reminders to the student that what he is doing must be changed.

A final strategy you can use is the most invasive one of the "direct redirections" because you actually say something out loud. If you are unable to make eye contact with him after a few attempts, but you are still working with a student across the room, you can say the student's name out loud. The key to making sure this is used effectively is the *way* that you say it. If you shout "JORDAN!" at the top of your lungs, you sadly stopped managing yourself, and your entire class now knows what is going on. Remember, this is not good because we never want to make one student's misbehavior a whole-class issue if it is possible to avoid it. Instead, you can say his name in the friendliest way possible, or with a firm tone (depending on the behavior you are seeing), and then respond with the two strategies described previously (a silent "Please stop … thank you!" or a firm look). If you say Jordan's name in the correct way and pair it with one of the two responses, it will get his attention without distracting too much of the rest of the class, while also changing his behavior. If you have built a relationship with the student, created a safe classroom climate, and said his name in a firm but well-meaning tone, this reprimand will not negatively hurt the student or the classroom climate.

Although this final example is a redirection that should be used in times of need, it should not be your first "go-to." It is important to remember always to begin with subtle steering, then move to the private redirection conversations, and finally use the public statements as a last resort. If you publicly call on students over and over again, then your classroom climate and relationships *will* be affected. Always go with the least invasive form of redirection when possible.

Implementing Consequences

All of the strategies explained thus far are going to fix the majority of the misbehavior you encounter. With the right structures in place, these will effectively work for you most of the time. With that said, there are going to be times when you do need to implement a consequence for student misbehaviors, but it can be difficult to figure out when to give those consequences and what they should look like. Even if you have thoroughly thought through what your expectations are, it can be hard as a beginning teacher to provide consequences because you do not *really* know what exactly you will and will not want your students to do. This is when your list of expectations and consequences (as discussed previously) will become your reference. This list will most likely morph and develop as the year goes on (which is okay, and sometimes very good!), but it will be incredibly helpful during your first weeks of school when you are still figuring out what you can live with and what you cannot.

All teachers will use different kinds of consequences depending on the classroom management system, teaching styles, and even clientele. As I mentioned previously, what is important is that you choose a consequence that fits these four criteria: consistent, reasonable, fair, and given with the end goal in mind of not having that misbehavior occur again. Since you have already planned a list of consequences that you may use, it is time to plan how you will implement those consequences. Always remember your goal is to get the student to alter his or her behavior. We do not want to ever overreact thus making the student who is misbehaving the center of attention and also acting in an unprofessional manner ourselves.

When giving a consequence to a student, it is important, just as in the previous scenarios, that you stay calm but speak or act confidently. Some consequences will be given verbally, such as "Natasha, I am sad you made that choice. You now owe me one minute of your passing period," or they will be given silently, such as moving a student's name over on the behavior chart. Either way, you do it in a respectful but firm manner, so you respect the student while also letting him or her know that you mean what you say. Jim Fay and David Funk, coauthors of *Teaching With Love and Logic*, also recommend giving consequences with empathy. "The effective teacher administers consequences with empathy and understanding, as opposed to anger and lecture" (p. 36). When you give consequences with confidence *and* empathy, students will know that "you mean business" while also knowing that you care about them and want them to do well. One essential reason for doing this is that even if the student you are correcting feels upset, the other students see you being fair and reasonable in your approach. By your doing it professionally, the corrected misbehaving student does not become an empathic figure for the rest of the class.

Since consistency is key with an effective consequence, we would recommend you also have some sort of tracking system to make sure that you follow through with what you say students must or must not do. Even if you provide a consequence with the perfect language or timing, if you do not follow through (like you forget to take away a minute of passing period, or you never move the student's name) students will not take your consequences seriously. This may be something you keep track of on a public behavior chart, or simply a note you jot down on a Post-it. No matter what it looks like, make sure that it works for you and helps you be a consistent teacher.

You also must be prepared for when a student may retaliate when you provide the consequence. For example, what if you take away a minute of passing period, but right after you give that consequence the student shouts, "BUT I DIDN'T DO ANYTHING!" This is one of the most difficult situations for first year teachers to deal with because they can easily choose two incorrect responses: allow the student to convince them to change their opinion, or make a rude, snarky, or threatening comment back that escalates the situation. If you allow a student to rudely retaliate and then get her way after she questions your decision, you are showing her and the rest of the class that you can easily be taken advantage of. This takes away any of the power that you had as the teacher, and students may no longer respect you as a leader. If you respond in the other way with a rude, snarky, or threatening response, your relationship with that student (and any other students who are listening) will be damaged, and it will be difficult to recover from that incident.

Instead of using those responses, there are a variety of other avenues you can take, depending on you, the student, and the situation. First, you could simply ignore the student and move on with the lesson. This would generally be the best response because it is the least invasive and lets the class know that you are ready to move on from the situation. This especially works if this student just needed to get her frustration out in a one-time outburst. With that said, there is a chance that this student was doing more than just letting off a bit of steam: She is trying to change the power dynamics in the classroom. If this is the case, a different response may be necessary so she knows that her behavior is not appropriate. You can do this in a gentle way by simply standing there quietly while waiting for her to calm down, or by saying a genuine, "I am sorry you feel that way." If you can tell that a firmer response is required, however, you can let her know that her behavior is inappropriate and explain why by saying, "Natasha, that was disrespectful and inappropriate. I cannot waste any more instruction time, but we can discuss it later if you would like." No matter which strategy you use (using the one that will work best with you and your students), always remember that the end goal is to work toward this misbehavior never occurring again.

When you are a teacher who follows through with what you say, there is always a chance that a student may not like this. Additionally, there is always a chance that this student will want everyone to know about *how much* he or she does not like it. The key to solving situations like these is to remember that there is no "perfect" response. Knowing and understanding the options you have for eliminating unwanted and extreme behavior is vital because in your first year you have not yet figured out what works. It may take a lot of trial and error, but with practice and experience, you will learn what even your toughest students will respond to.

For example, let's say you are continuing to have issues with Natasha. After you gave Natasha her first consequence for shouting, "BUT I DIDN'T DO ANYTHING," she stormed back to her seat, and on the way kicked a chair and growled, "I hate this class," under her breath. You decide to give her a minute to calm down, but you can tell that her behavior is continuing to escalate. She wants you, the class, and the whole school to know how angry she is. This is a key moment for you and your class, especially if this is at the beginning of the year. Natasha is testing your limits by continuing to disobey you, and the class is watching her to see what she (and even they) can get away with. If you do not want her behavior to be interpreted as something that is acceptable, it is time to respond with another consequence. Whether that is time in a "buddy room," a parent phone call home, a private conversation, or something else, this is where the "trial and error" comes into play. Choose what you think the best response is, and see what happens. If it works, great; if not, you know you need to try something different next time. Although situations like these are always tough, the good news is that generally speaking, once students know what your limits are as a teacher, they will follow within those guidelines and you will learn how to respond when they don't. There is a chance that at home or in another class, this behavior helps Natasha get what she wants. Once she learns it will not help her in *your* classroom, however, you may be amazed with how her behavior slowly turns around.

One final thought is that it is important to remember that not all consequences will work. What works with one student may not work with another. What works with one student may not even work with that same student the next day! Thus, make sure you continuously work on building relationships, because when you are close with a student the consequences will inherently mean more since they will be disappointed in themselves for letting you down. With that said, never forget that your ultimate goal should always be to build students' intrinsic motivation. Ultimately, you do not want them to follow directions because you "said so;" you want them to follow directions because they care about learning. Although that is much easier said than done, and although it is a craft that requires lessons full of authenticity and relevance, it is a good vision to keep in the back of your head as you work through those tough management moments.

Individual Case Study

Even with all of these techniques in place, there is still a chance that you will have one or two students who struggle with behavior. For our first example, let's pretend you are having an issue with just one student, Aaron. Even after using the multitude of strategies listed earlier, you are still consistently having the same problems with him: talking out, not completing work, messing around with classmates, violent outbursts, etc. What do you do?

First, if the behaviors do not seem to distract other students, your flexibility in dealing with this is quite great. This shows that you have created the classroom climate that you want, and it is truly just this one student who is having issues. If it were a larger group of students having issues, you would have to seriously consider pressing the "reset button," which is something that will be discussed later in the book.

Additionally, when working with students like Aaron, it is important to remember that making excuses will never ever help solve the problem. If you tell yourself that he has a tough home life, thus there is no way that you can get him to behave at school, you are doing him, the other students, and yourself a disservice. You must see the potential in him, because you are his teacher and you may be the only person in the school who actually believes in his ability to be a successful student.

We are going to walk you through the thought processes to take to figure out a way to help Aaron. Before we begin, though, you must know that *we are assuming you and Aaron have a good relationship.* If you do not, that needs to be a main focus as you problem-solve the situation. Recent research argues that teachers must begin to see classroom management as "an ongoing exercise in relationship building," especially for the most difficult students (Beaty-O'Ferrall, Green, & Hanna, 2010, p. 10). Remember, the success of your teaching relies on a foundation of great relationships with students.

Now, let's get back to the plan. To begin, you must ask yourself these three questions:

◆ When are most of the problems occurring?
◆ What am I doing that is perpetuating this problem?
◆ What can I do to help solve this problem?

The first thing you must be able to do is to reflect on Aaron. When are most of the problems occurring? If you are an elementary teacher, you think about time of day—morning or afternoon? Before math or during writing? After lunch or after specials? If you are a secondary teacher, you will need to think in shorter time chunks. Right after the student walks in? Ten minutes into lecture? During group work? There is also a chance the patterns reflect things that occur outside of school. For example, you may find that Aaron's roughest days occur when he spent the night at mom's house instead of dad's. You may need to keep track on a notepad or device to figure out when the issues start. Finding this pattern can be critical because it will provide a basis for planning your behavior intervention plan.

Once you find this pattern, you then think about how *you* may be negatively affecting the situation. If he is consistently starting his class off in a negative way, think about how you may be perpetuating this. Has your seating chart placed him in a location that he cannot be successful in? Are your beginning-of-class structures tight enough for him to follow (no "down time," must work on bellringer, etc.)? Is he understanding the work that you are asking him to do? Remember to always have the mindset that you are the one who has the most influence on this student's behavior, so be honest with yourself about ways that you may be causing the misbehavior.

After you think through these types of questions, you then process through how you *can* help him. This part of the plan can be difficult for first year teachers because your tool belt will not be as full of resources as other teachers' down the hallway. Additionally, you may realize that your student needs more help than you can provide, like access to a counselor or social worker. Thus, do not be afraid to reach out to resources in and outside of your school for advice. Find a trusted colleague and ask him or her for advice. See if your principal, mentor, or instructional coach can guide you to resources. Also, feel free to look for ideas in books, articles, or online. In working with students like Aaron, there will never be an easy answer to your problems. You must have the ability to critically think about the situation, and either come up with or find solutions that help Aaron find success in your room.

The "What If" Situations

We have worked through what you should do for each of the 99 percent of behavior issues that you may have, but we know you are still left with the "what ifs." What if a student throws a desk? What if a student runs out of the classroom? What if two students get in a fight? These are the scenarios that can really distract you when you are planning how to run your classroom. Yes, it is necessary to have procedures in place to deal with these, and it is scary to think about something like this happening. But it is critical that you focus on the "subtle-steering" and "direct redirection" techniques the majority of the time because if you do them right, your "what if" situations will be few and far between (if ever).

Now we know what some of you may be thinking. "You don't understand; I work at *that* school." Or, "Inner-city students have such hard home lives that I know there will be physical altercations every day. That is just the kind of kids I will have." "The teachers have warned me about what my students will be like. I know not to smile before Thanksgiving." We are just letting you know that if this is what you are thinking, you are setting yourself and your students up for failure. If you think that this type of behavior is going to be normal because you work with "those kids," then you are already making excuses (and we already warned you about those earlier!).

Previously in the book we asked you to make sure you believed in two things: Every student matters and every student has the capacity to learn. We were not just talking about learning in an academic sense; we also meant learning in a behavioral and emotional sense too. You must believe that all of your students have the capacity to look like learners in your classroom, no matter the

> You must believe that all of your students have the capacity to look like learners in your classroom, no matter the climate of the school that you are in. If you need to be the exception in your building, so be it. That is what is best for students.

climate of the school that you are in. If you need to be the exception in your building, so be it. That is what is best for students.

So what do you do when a "what if" situation occurs? These moments can be scary to think about, but with the right planning, you can be ready for a variety of situations. First, you must be familiar with your school's policies and procedures when such extreme incidents occur. Generally, your school has protocol for you to follow if a "what if" situation, such as a fight or a student bringing in a weapon, occurs. These are the moments where you *should* and *must* use those resources, so it is important for you to know what the steps are that you must take in this situation. You can find these out either in your school handbook or by simply talking to an administrator. Also, during these types of moments, you *should* and *must* call for help. These are the extreme moments where an administrator should be involved, and as a teacher (and especially a first year teacher) you should not have to handle them on your own.

Repairing and Rebuilding

We want to begin this section by reminding you that even though we are teachers, we are all human and we will all make mistakes.

Never ever be afraid to apologize if you realize that you chipped away at one of those relationships. Remember the scenario described earlier where you gave Natasha a consequence for misbehavior you thought you saw, but then she responded with "But I didn't do anything!" Although there is a good chance she did do something, there is also a chance you got it wrong. If that is the case, Natasha will be mad and frustrated until you reconcile with her. Even if you make a mistake, if you go to that student, admit your mistake and sincerely apologize for what occurred, your bond can be repaired. For example, after talking with Natasha and realizing she genuinely did not do anything wrong, you could say, "Natasha, I am so sorry for accusing you of doing something you did not do. Even though I am a teacher, I still make mistakes and I appreciate your willingness to discuss what happened." As long as your apology is genuine, there is no wrong way to do it. Just make it a priority to admit when you do make a mistake because it will protect and nurture the relationship you had created by repairing the damage you caused.

Always remember that the best way to get in the last word is to apologize. Great teachers seldom need to repair, but they are always working to repair. Other teachers need to repair but they do so infrequently. For example, a truly outstanding teacher says to his class Tuesday morning, "I am sorry I seemed short yesterday, I wasn't feeling well. I apologize." If the teacher is truly outstanding the students do not say, "That's okay," they say, "We don't even know what you are talking about." If in doubt, repair.

> **Always remember that the best way to get in the last word is to apologize.**

A Final Note

As a final note, always remember to not be ashamed when behavior management does not go as hoped or planned. Students are people, and people are complicated. During your first year, you learn and learn a lot. We teach our students to not be afraid of failure, so we want you to not be afraid as well. You may have teachers in your school who will not be nice about your management woes, but if that is the case, they either forgot how hard the first year is, are trying to make themselves feel better by putting you down, or are even hiding insecurities about their own management practices by pointing out your flaws.

No matter what anyone says, always remember that things can and will get better. Use all of the strategies described in this book and any that you find online, hear from a colleague, or observe in another classroom. If you have truly tried every strategy you can think of with a student and things are continually getting worse, that is when you unashamedly *ask for help*. Whether you ask help from a colleague, supervisor, or even a teacher you personally had, always remember you are not alone. Most likely, whomever you reach out to will vividly remember their "bad days," and will be more than willing to help turn yours around.

There are very few things in the classroom that someone hasn't figured out. Later in the book we talk about how to find those people and then be able to use them to give you guidance when needed. Also, always keep in mind that we are in the improvement business, we are not in the perfection business. Effective teachers are very demanding of themselves. That is one of the things that make them so special. Make sure, however, that being demanding of yourself does not mean you are afraid to reach out for help or make mistakes. Remember that asking for help is actually a sign of strength, not a sign of weakness. Doing things like this also makes others more comfortable coming to you for guidance. You are in your first year. Just knowing you do not know the answer is a tremendous first step toward finding it.

Section III

Working with Adults

9

Working with Administrators

When you made the choice to be a teacher, one of the reasons was the opportunity to influence and impact young people. You had a desire to work with students, and that was likely one of the driving forces, if not *the* driving force, in choosing this special profession. As you moved forward throughout your teacher preparation program, some reluctance may have occurred because you started worrying about classroom management. What do I do if the students do not do what I ask? How do I deal with the most challenging student in my class? What if they don't like me?!

Each of these worries centers around the relationships with the students in our classroom. And this is a natural part of becoming a first year teacher. Being able to have a high-functioning classroom is essential to being effective. That is one of the reasons such a large percentage of this book focuses on classroom management, student behavior, structure, lesson planning, etc. If you are not able to be successful in these areas, teaching can be overwhelming, frustrating, and exhausting. But working successfully with students is not the only relationship that comes into play. We also need to be able to interact productively with the adults in and out of our school.

This is a delicate section to write. Centering on students is something all teachers have in common. Though the classes and clientele may vary, every teacher has teacher-pleaser students as well as those who challenge our patience and abilities. We knew this before we stepped into the classroom the first day. Some schools have more higher-needs students and others have fewer, but it is something that every teacher faces. The adults we interact with can vary tremendously from school to school, grade level to grade level, department to department, etc. Our aim is to help everyone regardless of the dynamic they are facing.

Administrative Support

Depictions of principals often tend to make them seem quite clumsy or even oafish on television or in the movies. When we think of the school leader in *Ferris Bueller's Day Off* it may cause us to chuckle at the generalization of how principals can be depicted. You also most likely had several principals when you were in school. Some of them may have projected an image that made us afraid of them. Others might have seemed to only interact with students when they were in trouble or doing something wrong. Some of us may have had little interaction with our principal and others may have had regular contact. In some schools we may even wonder what it is the principal actually does.

Generalizing about principals is one thing. But now a specific administrator is your supervisor. Potentially they hired you, evaluate you, and are in a role to support you. It isn't about principals as a whole, it is about your particular administrator(s). Being able to build a positive relationship with them is essential. Being supportive of them is also a component of teaching.

In many schools the principal is very involved in the hiring process. This is good because it means they chose you to be a part of their school. That is a plus already! You were selected because of your talent and potential. In most cases, if the principal didn't want you there, you would not be in the school. Instead you were chosen to be in your role. However, like any profession, skills of principals can vary and the way people in any organization view their "bosses" can be quite different from person to person.

You might compare the relationship between a principal and the teachers in their school to that of a teacher and the students in their classroom. Some of the students in your class are always prepared, work very hard and consistently do their best. Additionally, the skill sets of the students in any class can be widely varying. Some of the students in your class need little direction. Others need your assistance in order to be successful and they welcome it when it is offered. However, there may be a few who are more rebellious or resistant to your guidance or even support. And, as you well know, there may be some who immediately get defensive or even outright aggressive if the teacher attempts to assist them or correct their behavior. And, as you can recall from being a student, the skills of the teachers can vary quite a bit. Some teachers struggle to get the students to behave appropriately and others make it seem quite easy. There are some teachers all of the students hold in great regard, and others who may have more mixed reviews. This may parallel the relationship between teachers and their principal.

If principals are highly effective, they are probably quite respected in their school by the vast majority of the teachers and parents. If they are very ineffective, they may have few supporters and little respect from others in and out of the school. And, of course, there are many school leaders who have an ability level that falls somewhere in between. It is very important though that you as a new teacher work to establish a relationship with everyone in your school, and that starts with the administrators.

> **It is very important though that you as a new teacher work to establish a relationship with everyone in your school, and that starts with the administrators.**

If your leaders are the best of the best, that is easy. They will seek you out for personal conversations, offer to help on a regular basis, and visit your classroom early and often to praise and support you. They make it easy to value them. Your peers in the school will speak highly of them and it is easy for you to join the chorus.

Other leaders, though, may be viewed through a varying lens. Obviously if a principal suspended a student, that child's parent may have a tainted view. Similarly, if a principal had to reprimand a staff member, that teacher may have a more negative opinion.

As a new teacher, it is not your task to sort these dynamics out. Instead it is to consistently take a positive approach and seek out opportunities to support and interact with your school administrators. Being a team player is important to helping school dynamics and is a role we must assume as we start our career. This will be addressed more in the next section, but it is important to not join individuals or a group that may speak negatively toward school or district administrators. There is no benefit to that and it does nothing to help the school and our own mindset. Always keep in mind that principals do the best they know how. The job is very complex and there are so many different perspectives to deal with. A high school teacher may be able to logically explain why their planning period should be the final hour of the day, but if we step back and think, not everyone can have that time off, because then what would we do with the students! It is much easier to criticize a leader than it is to be one. Work hard to build relationships with others before we need relationships with them.

10

Working with Peers

Peer Support

As we know, in every classroom there are students who make our lives easy and others who take more energy. There are students who want to do what is right and others who want to test the limits. If we think about it, these students become adults. Some of these adults become teachers. Just like the skills and attitudes of students vary, the skills and attitudes of adults cut just as wide a swathe. In every school there is a large number of teachers who work hard each day, have a positive attitude and consistently make a difference with students. Seek these people out. Learn from them. Steal ideas from them—if they are really good they will love to share with you. Draw from their experience and their energy. If you have a chance, go in their classrooms on your plan time and observe them. Learn from the best of the best. The better they are, the more welcoming they will be. Remember that.

Hopefully some of these people are in your hallway, at your grade level, in your department or team, share a common plan time or lunch period. Maybe one of them is your mentor and can become a trusted colleague. If you can link up with them, milk it for all it is worth. It will make your first year—and the rest of your time at that school—much more pleasurable. If you can find that special person or persons, we call them empowerers, full speed ahead! This is addressed in the following chapter. However, we would be remiss to not issue a gentle warning that there might be others in the school who do not have the same altruistic perspective of teaching every day of the school year.

We probably remember from when we were students that some teachers had a countdown on their chalkboard of how many days of school remained in the year. When you were a student you probably thought that was for you. Upon reflection it may have been for them. Did you ever have a teacher who warned the class that they were in a bad mood that day? Did you ever have one do that more than once?

Watch and listen to how the teachers in your school greet their students when they arrive at their class. Do some smile warmly and issue a personal welcome every day regardless of their mood? Do you have others who do it depending on day of the week, how they are feeling or how much they like the class? Have you ever seen a teacher who doesn't even smile every day when the students arrive at their door? Which one are you? Which one do you want to be? Which one do you want to associate with?

Teaching is a very rewarding profession. No question. It is also very intense and draining. Making sure that you are in a positive frame of mind each day is essential. People tend to interact with those who have similar abilities and belief systems. Positive people are drawn to others with similar approaches. Negative individuals are much more comfortable around others who want to complain and whine.

> **Making sure that you are in a positive frame of mind each day is essential.**

As a new teacher, many groups are working to have you join them. If there are some constant complainers, they will try griping around you. If you chime in, they have you. They want to find others who feel they are overworked, underpaid, and unappreciated. Do not let yourself be recruited by this crew! They are really good at drawing people in and they love to go after the fresh recruits. Think about this in an elementary school. Have you ever known a teacher who cannot wait to tell next year's teacher about how horrible their students are going to be? We have to realize that not only is that person rooting against next year's teacher, they are even hoping to ruin their summer by causing them to worry all break. But, more importantly, they are even rooting against the students. They are hoping they will not learn anything next year either.

Our peers can be incredibly supportive and the vast majority are. But there can be some who do not always choose that path. We need to be nice to everyone, but emulate certain ones. It is essential to having a wonderful inaugural year in teaching. With that heads up, now find those special people who help build your confidence on a daily basis.

11

The Empowerers

The Empowerers and Navigating the Waters

During your first year, you are going to work unbelievably hard to attempt to make sure things go smoothly every day. You will spend hours planning lessons. Each day will be spent building relationships with your students. You will also work hard to smile and greet everyone you come in contact with because you want to be a positive influence in your classroom and in your building. Then, the unexpected will occur.

No matter how hard we humans try, at some point every one of us will end up with one of those unexpected terrible, horrible, no good, very bad days. Those days might be caused by a lesson not going well, a student interaction that did not end the way you had hoped, a negative teacher, or an upset parent. When these situations arise, what do you do?

For a while you can work through these ups and downs alone. Hopefully at first you can reach out to family and friends for guidance. However, eventually it is beneficial to find another expert educator to turn to in those times of strife or frustration. Someone who has a similar educational philosophy, but more importantly, someone you can trust to be there for you. We call these special educators your "empowerers." Since this is an original word, we are going to include a definition. An empowerer is someone who builds confidence, happiness, and strength in another. True empowerers are precious gifts but where can we find them?

An empowerer is someone who builds confidence, happiness, and strength in another.

Finding Your Empowerer

The work day(s) before school starts is a perfect time for the first year teacher to begin this empowerer search! The year is new and everyone is excited, including yourself. Even if you are a bit nervous, there are people in your faculty who are so looking forward to meeting you! New teachers always help to rejuvenate the passion of a school. Many people are going to be drawn to that and will want to help you in any way that they can and also learn from the knowledge you bring to the school. Use this time to not only plan your classroom, but also get to know the people in your building.

You will probably start off interacting with teachers from your grade level, team, or department. Typically you also have chances to interact with others who are new to the school. This is a perfect time to sit back, listen, and observe. Take mental notes: Who is the person who brings positive energy to the situation? Who seems excited about the new school year? Identifying individuals who can assist when needed and provide the big picture when you feel discouraged is very important for new teachers. Empowerers are consistently positive and the type of people you want to associate and interact with regularly.

You may find your empowerer your very first day on the job. Ideally, your empowerer would be someone assigned to you officially as a mentor. But what about those who may not end up so lucky? Let us pretend that you are placed on a team or in a department where things are not as supportive as you had hoped. If your empowerers are not handed to you, then you are going to have to start searching for them. You have to find like-minded people to lift you up and those like-minded people may not be in the classroom adjacent to yours. So how do you find them?

There are four places you could look: your school, your district, outside professional development, and social media. We mentioned the preservice days, but what about all the other meetings? Take those as opportunities to sit by and meet people outside of your grade level, content area, or team. What about others who share a lunch with you or have a common plan time? Most teachers have to serve on a building-level committee. These committee meetings are great ways to meet people who you may not see on a regular basis. These people could be a source of optimism and support.

Use any district event as a way to do the same thing. Whole district curriculum-writing groups, serving on a district committee, or in-service days are a few examples of ways to interact with people outside of your building. Usually whole district meetings have break times for lunch, so feel free to go with people from other buildings. See if anyone you meet at these meetings could be a source of strength or support for you.

Outside professional development is another option. Ask other teachers or your principal about conferences in the area or state. Use Google to find some based on your interests and schedule. Sometimes getting a sub your first year can be scary. Try to find conferences that occur on the weekend such as Edcamps. The reason we encourage you to try and attend conferences is that people who are passionate, care, and try, flock to them. These conferences can be huge learning experiences but also unbe-lievably rejuvenating.

If, for whatever reason, you do not have any of those opportu-nities, there is one last resort. And honestly, we may have saved the best for last: Twitter. Make a Twitter account (right now!). There are so many amazing educators all over the Twitter universe. Just search "education" or #NTChat (New Teacher Chat). Thousands of people, articles, lesson plans, and inspira-tional quotes will appear in seconds. All of these can be used as constant reminders as to why you became a teacher and why your job is so important.

Keep in mind that everyone needs empowerers and you just might end up being someone's empowerer too! If this happens, not only will you go to them to brainstorm solutions to problems within your classroom, but they will also come to you. Just remember that they should fill your cup much more than empty it, and vice versa. Work together to create a safe and positive educational relationship that will get you through the hard times and help you celebrate the great ones.

> **Work together to create a safe and positive educational relationship that will get you through the hard times and help you celebrate the great ones.**

What About Everyone Else?

Empowerers will always be your number one "go-to" when things tend to get hard, but the other people in your building can play huge roles in helping you develop as an educator. These people all have various skills that they bring to the table, and many of these individuals have something that you can learn and draw from. For example, a teacher on your team might not be a strong classroom manager, but the way they organize field trips is impeccable. Work with them to learn that skill. The band teacher may not teach your subject matter, but you have heard through the grapevine that their technology integration is jaw dropping. Although these teachers may not be your empowerers, appreciate them for the gifts they bring.

Fortunately for you the majority of the teachers in your school have insights and ideas that will help you grow professionally. And the majority of them are more than happy to share, especially if you ask for their assistance. Unfortunately there may be a sliver of your peers that do not always have an altruistic purpose. This final category of teacher might be called the 2 percent. They exist in the majority of schools. If we give them too much power, the 2 percent can certainly damage the morale of the school. The 2 percent are often the teachers who complain the loudest and most frequently. They also, ironically, may be the ones who work the least. The 2 percent can sometimes be seen sleeping or texting throughout staff meetings (if they even come). They may even be known for secretly wanting others, including the students, to fail so they can have more proof as to why they cannot succeed in their classroom.

These teachers are going to be negative, they are going to complain, and they may try to get you to do the same. Your one and only goal is to always be nice to them but never join in with them. Stay positive and strong because it is best for the students in your school. Learn to avoid this 2 percent and stick close to your empowerers. Through them you will grow to become the teacher you want to be and impact your students positively every single day.

12

Don't Be Afraid to Repair: Students, Co-Workers, Principal

As mentioned earlier, you are going to work very hard to build and repair relationships with individual students. But what do you do if you mess up in front of an entire class one day? What do you do if you find out a co-worker is mad at you? What do you do if you are grading papers in your room at 6 p.m. and suddenly realize you forgot about the staff meeting that was supposed to be right after school?

As human beings, and teachers, we are going to make mistakes. Those mistakes might be in the classroom with a room full of students watching you. That mistake might end up being an email you sent that was taken the wrong way. You might upset a parent, a co-worker, or your principal. In situations like these some people are more tempted to slide the issue under the rug, ignore it, or run from it. Those responses may seem easier, but we are going to encourage you to take a different approach. Admitting faults or mistakes can be difficult for anyone. But in this

> **Admitting faults or mistakes can be difficult for anyone. But in this profession, and in life, we cannot be afraid to repair. And the sooner the better!**

profession, and in life, we cannot be afraid to repair. And the sooner the better!

Our first example is going to show you how to repair with an entire class. Imagine that you are doing an activity with your eighth hour on a Friday. Not only is it Friday, but it just so happens to be the Friday before Halloween. It is the last class of the day and they start off a little squirrely. You begin by giving a few redirects to a couple overly chatty students. You then try to compliment good behavior from the students who really are working diligently. However, as the hour continues the volume rises and more and more people seem to be getting off task. You see a pencil fly across the room. Then a couple students try to make a three-point shot into the trashcan with their scraps of paper. Your patience is waning and you finally ask for the entire class's attention. It takes what seems like several minutes for everyone to stop talking and turn their focus to you. By this point you are so frustrated that you sternly tell them to put everything away, put their heads on their desks and sit there in silence the last few minutes of the period. They leave when the bell rings and immediately you start to feel anxious. You worry all weekend about how you should address the situation and class on Monday.

When reflecting on what happened, you feel uncomfortable with how you handled the situation. Yes, they were misbehaving, but there is a chance you were too. You know that when Monday comes and eighth hour arrives, you need to repair for your unprofessional actions.

On Monday, the students trickle into the room and after the bell rings you let them know you have something you need to say. "I want to apologize for what happened Friday in class. I am so sorry that I raised my voice inappropriately and ended the fun activity we were doing. I handled the situation and more importantly handled myself unprofessionally. Secondly, I need to let you know that my feelings were hurt by your behavior on Friday. I felt disrespected when you ignored me and threw things around our classroom. We both need to choose alternative behaviors in the future."

According to Susan Scott in *Fierce Conversations* (2004), apologizing and sharing how you felt are two important aspects of repairing relationships. In this scenario, you did both. First, you apologized for your behavior. Yes, the students accelerated it, but admitting that you did not handle the situation correctly makes this discussion feel like less of an attack on the students. Next, you shared your feelings. Instead of saying their behavior was "terrible," "ridiculous," or "out of line," you became vulnerable and softened the situation. Words like that put students on the defensive and make them tune you out or attack back.

An additional option that you can choose to use is allowing your students to share their feelings as well (Scott, 2002). This entirely depends on your ability to respond appropriately when you may not get the answer that you want. Thus, only use this strategy when you feel comfortable and confident enough to facilitate and listen.

One of the most common reactions when you apologize to your class or individual is for a student to say, "We have never had a teacher apologize before." This is a great reassurance that you handled it correctly and now you and the student(s) are ready to move forward.

A second situation is how to repair with a co-worker. Imagine that you found out a teacher is upset because of an email you sent. You remember writing the email during a time of frustration, so you open it back up to refresh your memory. After rereading it, you see how it could have been taken the wrong way and hurt feelings. Instead of avoiding the situation, you must be the bigger person and seek that teacher out. Do not send another email. Find them and say: "Jenna, I just wanted to apologize to you about that email. It was written during a time of frustration and I never intended to hurt your feelings. I am beyond sorry." Short and simple. The sooner this conversation happens the better. If you let them sit in their feelings for too long your apology might not seem as sincere or they may be slower to forgive.

Finally, what do you do if you need to apologize with a supervisor, like if you missed a faculty meeting on accident? Never wait for the principal to come find you. Again, be the one to initiate contact. The second you realize you missed the meeting, email, then go directly to your principal and apologize. "Dr. Boyer, I was in my classroom grading papers and just realized I missed the faculty meeting after school. I am so sorry! Please let me know what I missed and if there is anything I need to do to make up for my absence. Again, I am so sorry that I missed the meeting." If you still feel a twinge of guilt the next morning, feel free to go to their office first thing in the morning with another apology.

13

Parents: Friend Not Foe

One aspect of being a teacher that you may not have much experience in is working with parents. Unless you had the chance during your teacher preparation program, you may have had little or no contact with parents. Now that you are a teacher this can be scary or intimidating. And, if you listen to colleagues, some of them love to tell stories about challenges they have had over their career. Our goal is to make sure you get started in the right direction.

The Best They Know How

No matter where you are located or what school you are in, the parents in that community have one thing in common: They all do the best they know how. That does not mean they do the best *you* know how. You may have come from a loving upper-middle-class nuclear family with 2.5 children and caring and supportive parents

> No matter where you are located or what school you are in, the parents in that community have one thing in common: They all do the best they know how.

who are still very happily married. You also may not have. Either way, make sure you are aware of the assumptions you have about families and parenting. No matter what your background is, you will most likely have students who come from families that function differently from what you are used to.

Just because you may have a different opinion about "good parents" does not mean that parents who act otherwise care less. It does not mean that they are not trying. No matter what the circumstances are, the students come from parents who love them and do the best they know how. We must always keep that in mind. They are just like you in that they want what is best for their children.

Interestingly enough, interacting with parents can oftentimes enable us to have so much more patience with our students. When we get frustrated with a student's attitude or behavior, sometimes meeting the parent causes us to reflect: "Boy, that makes sense why he doesn't know how to control his anger!" Of course we would never say this out loud, but knowing a student's family and background can help us by providing a context from which the student comes. This context helps us see that what one student finds normal and appropriate may be different from what we find "normal" and "appropriate."

Build Relationships Before You Need Relationships

If we wait to hear from parents, or wait to contact them only when something is going wrong, many times the only contact we have with them is negative. When a parent's sole interaction with a teacher or school is negative, they will understandably be much less likely to want to interact with the school. Thus we need to initiate positive contact so we get better and more comfortable with communicating with parents in case issues arise that must be discussed.

If possible, make phone calls to parents/families before the school year starts. Or at least send them a letter or email. Reach out to them and tell them how excited you are to work with their children. Make them feel warm and invited. Do this at the beginning of the year, or even before the year starts, to help them have a positive frame of mind about you and the school year.

Also, if your school has an open house night or back to school night, use this opportunity to make the parents/families feel welcome. This should not just be about your curriculum, grading policy or instructional practices. We have to make sure we use this occasion to make the parents feel that you are going to take care of their children. This is at the core of what all parents want.

Overall, remember that parents so seldom hear good things from schools and teachers. If you can be the person who does these things, you will be able to establish credibility prior to needing it. Even if you are noticing an issue with a student early on, it is best to try to quickly contact their parents about something positive before calling them about that student's issues. By doing this in advance a teacher can have more credibility with that parent when they must have the tougher conversation.

What Do I Say When I Call a Parent?

Learning how to start a conversation can be very comforting as we move forward with parent contact and phone calls. Here is some insight from the book *Dealing With Difficult Parents, 2nd Edition* (Whitaker & Fiore, 2016), which provides a great deal of information in communication with all parents, especially the most challenging ones.

Practicing a particular approach prior to doing something that you are unfamiliar with or even uncomfortable with can be very helpful in building up your confidence. For example, you were probably terribly nervous the first time you decided to call someone up and ask him or her out on a date. You might have practiced what you wanted to say in your head a million times before you made that call. You may have even written down what you anticipated saying and added extra notes of a couple of other topics to bring up in case the conversation fizzled. Once you decided how you wanted to start the conversation, it gave you a little more confidence when you started to actually dial the number. This same thing can be true if we are not used to initiating contact with parents. Just like teaching a lesson, preparation can be very beneficial.

Positive or negative, we always want to start all of our parental phone calls in the same manner. Everyone can meld an approach that works best for them, but having a place to start can go a long way toward building our skills. One way to start every phone contact, positive or negative, could be with this language: "Hi, Mrs. Johnson, this is Tom Walker, Kevin's science teacher at Smith Middle School. I am sorry to bother you at work (or home), but …" Consistently having a professional tone with either good news or not so good news can help establish a productive relationship with each of the parents we communicate with.

Every conversation is going to sound different, but we wanted to give you an example of how to give positive news and how to give negative news.

> Positive news: "Hi, Mrs. Johnson, this is Tom Walker, Kevin's science teacher at Smith Middle School. I am so sorry to bother you at work, but I wanted to call and let you know that Kevin got 100 percent on his science test yesterday! I was so excited for him because I could tell he worked so incredibly hard studying this past week." The parent will respond in a variety of ways, but you can always end the conversation with, "Have a wonderful day."

Positive phones calls can be short and sweet, but they make everyone's day just a little bit better. Even after rough days, making a positive phone call can remind you that you *do* have great students who deserve recognition. And always keep in mind that every time you use praise, at least two people feel better and one of them is you.

Even after rough days, making a positive phone call can remind you that you *do* have great students who deserve recognition.

> Negative news: "Hi, Mrs. Johnson, this is Tom Walker, Kevin's science teacher at Smith Middle School. I am so sorry to bother you at work, but I am calling to let you know that Kevin has failed his last science test and I am beginning to worry about him. He started out the year so strong, but has slowly stopped

turning in assignments. I truly believe in Kevin, and know he can be successful in my class. I would love to work with you to help get him back on the right track."

Negative phone calls may be a bit scary, even for the most seasoned teachers. Even with this fear, here are three things you can do when making them that will help it be a productive conversation. The first is to be direct about the issue at hand. Get to the point quickly and emphasize that you are worried about the student. The second is to try and note something positive about the student. "Alicia is so artistically gifted but is struggling to stay focused when we have to take notes in art. I do not want this one thing to hinder her grade because her projects are phenomenal!" Lastly, you must let the parents know that their child can be successful and that you want to work *with* them to help their child succeed. By focusing on the future it can ease any strain on events that may have happened up to this point. Rather than coming to an understanding of events up until now, it is easy to agree that both the teacher and parent want a different result in the future.

Most of the time, if you state the issue quickly, mention something the child is good at, and talk about finding a solution together, the parents will be open to talking or continuing to listen. These conversations can be very beneficial and could immediately end the issues you are seeing in your classroom. Parents might talk to their child about the problem, they may give you an idea that works for them at home, or they will possibly give you permission to handle the situation however you see fit.

It can be helpful if you come into the phone call with one or two options of how you would like to handle the issue at hand. Let's go back to the situation with Kevin failing his last science test. After you had shared your initial message, there will come a point in the conversation where you can say, "I have a couple ideas about how we could start fixing this situation and would love your feedback. First, I am available Tuesday and Thursday before school. If Kevin would like to come in for some one-on-one tutoring I would love to work with him. Secondly, I do allow test retakes. I can email you the assignments Kevin needs to do in order to retake the tests. Do either of those options sound like something you or Kevin might be interested in?"

With the Alicia example, you are really just letting the parents know this is an issue and if it does not get resolved things could get a little more serious. "I am going to try to resolve this by moving Alicia to the front of the room during notes so that I can keep a better eye on her. If that does not work I am going to place her in the 'safe seat' in the back of my room until she can prove to be successful during note time. I just wanted to keep you in the loop about what I am seeing and will let you know if and when this issue gets resolved."

The scenarios are different but both involve you communicating the issue clearly, voicing to the parents that you want their child to be successful, then letting them know options they have or how you are handling the situation right now. Another tip if we have to deliver bad news to a parent is to try to make sure you contact the parent before their child gets to them. As you can remember when being a child yourself, once in a while when they do something wrong, children may possibly taint the story with a slightly slanted perspective. Then if the parent contacts us, we may feel more defensive. However, if we contact them first it can be helpful to establish our perspective before the student shares a differing viewpoint. Always keep in mind that that phone is our best friend, unless it is ringing.

Even when you use the more professional protocols, there may be times when these difficult phone calls do not go as we as we would hope. Parents may be angry with us, frustrated with their child, or with life in general. Sorting that out can be a challenge. But remember, with parents just like with students and co-workers, the best way to get in the last word is to apologize. If the parent is upset we can say, "I am sorry that happened." This is not an admission of guilt, but it is a way to show empathy and allow the relationship to continue to move forward. Saying "I was wrong" is powerful but only appropriate when you truly were wrong. Saying, "I am sorry that happened" is a more universal way to repair. Even if it is completely the student who was incorrect—cheating on a test, bullying a peer, etc.—you are sorry it happened and this can be a productive way to build the relationship no matter who initiates the contact.

Section IV

Continuing to Reflect, Refine, and Grow on Your Journey

Mid-Flight Corrections

Though you may have spent a great deal of time and effort preparing and planning for the school year, it is impossible to predict every situation and scenario that you will face. We may visualize our procedures and set up our classroom in the best manner for things we could foresee. However, then something happens. And that something is the first days of school. The students show up and things do not always go as we had envisioned. You may feel a sense of panic, but what you should actually feel is a sense of normal. Every teacher faces these issues. If you did not feel like there were things you need to change then something really is wrong. There are differing levels of alterations you can make. You may want to carefully think through the options before deciding what is actually needed. You need to act, but you do not want to overly act, or even worse, overly react. Let's take a look at what our options are.

Every day effective teachers reflect on how things went in their classroom. We think about where we stood, the tone of our voice, whether our instructions and explanations were clear, etc. When we decide to make a change in things, there are really two levels to consider. One we call tweaking and the other is the reset button. Both are valuable but also take different approaches. Let's look at each one.

Tweaking: Be Your Own Control Group

Let's imagine that Mr. Johnson is not pleased with how his third hour class has been starting. The students come in quite boisterously and it seems like a "battle royale" just to get them to focus. His four other classes, however, have a very different tone. In those, students seem to understand his expectations easily, which allows him to happily stand at the front of the room and smile as the students arrive. He can tell that some strategies he is using are effective because four of his classes are going well. With that third hour, though, something must change.

Mr. Johnson considers talking to the entire class about behaving more appropriately. Though after further reflection, he realizes that it is not the *entire* class, so he doesn't know who a class-wide discussion would really benefit. He could also let students individually know that he is upset with them, but it is more than two or three students, so that would take lots of time, and he doesn't know how much that would help his relationship. Rather than telling his students explicitly that their behavior needs to change, he could instead change his behavior first and see if that makes a difference. Starting tomorrow, Mr. Johnson has decided to greet his third period at the door, catch them before they enter the classroom, and smile while kindly welcoming students and asking them to start reading the directions on the whiteboard so they know what to complete.

This strategy is called a tweak. A tweak is when you change your behavior, but do not need to inform/announce to the students that anything is changing. Even though your students will realize you may be implementing different expectations, you approach it in such a positive tone that they won't realize the decision came from a reaction to their behavior. Instead you tweak *your* behavior in order to prevent misbehavior that was occurring previously.

One benefit of tweaking is that you can do this an unlimited number of times during a school year and even over the course of your career. And you should. Just like a football team at halftime, we need to continuously assess and, if necessary, adjust what we are doing. Let's pretend that Mr. Johnson was finding success with his new approach toward his third hour class, but he was still having issues with students chatting after they sat down. It is time for another tweak. Maybe he realizes that he had not changed the seating arrangement for about two months, so the next day when students walked in, he reminded them of his expectations and also told them to find their new seat quietly. If a student asks Mr. Johnson why he switched them around, he simply says, "I feel like it was time to shake things up a bit," or, "This new seating arrangement will help me form new discussion groups for the next unit," since, as you know, we don't need to tell students the real reason why we are changing things up.

Just like this secondary example, an elementary teacher may sense a dramatically different feel for the students at different points in the day (e.g., after lunch, recess, or physical education vs. during the highly structured literacy stations or writing block). In any of these situations, elementary teachers can and should also tweak things to help improve the issues that are at hand. Maybe you play soft music "randomly" when students come in from their specials class, although *you* know that you purposefully play the music on P.E. days. No matter what tweak you make, always monitor the behavior changes to see which one(s) are most effective. By doing this you develop your own control group. This does not mean any one way always works (because you never know when you will have to tweak a tweak!), but you can continue to subtly move students and your classroom in a positive direction.

With all of this said, there may be occasions that require a more dramatic change; a change that does require more specific and direct communication with students. Remember that tweaking can and should occur on a regular basis as needed. Our next option, when larger-scale changes are needed, is called the reset button.

The Reset Button

As much as you prepare for your first year, there are times when things may start to go wrong. Things might begin going awry the second week, the second month, or the second semester. You can always tweak, but what if it is not just one issue that is happening? What if you feel like you are slowly losing control of your classroom? What if you find things are getting worse and not better? What if you start regretting a couple of the rules you implemented at the beginning of the year? You might try to plow on at first, hoping the kids are just in a funk, or maybe you are just "in a mood," but that will only work for so long. What do you do? How do you know if you are at that point?

It's time to reset when … it is October and kids are starting to use the pencil sharpener too much. By too much, we mean that during your lesson you look up and it is like a party by the pencil sharpener. You even have kids back there trying to sharpen their pens. In addition, students are blurting out answers instead of raising their hands to the questions you pose. By blurting out, we mean that Martese and Raquel think it is hilarious to yell out "Twenty-one" to every single question you ask. After a five-minute passing period students are asking to use the bathroom two minutes into class even though they know they have to wait and go after the lesson is over. Kids are starting to get out of their seats whenever they want to throw things away, then they hit a kid on their way to the trashcan. You hope that ignoring all of this will make it go away, but things seem to just be escalating. After a rough Friday you have decided enough is enough and you want your classroom back.

You start to think of tweaks that you want to make, but realize that it has gone too far. For whatever reason you can no longer be the teacher you wanted to be. If any or all of these things are occurring then it is time to hit the "reset button." The differences between a "tweak" and the "reset button" are big:

1. Although there is no limit to how many times you can "tweak," you really only have one (maybe two) "reset buttons."
2. "Tweaks" are small adjustments the teacher makes to change their own behavior. "Reset buttons" are communicated to the class, and they are large changes that will require students to adjust their behavior.
3. "Tweaks" are greeting students at the door with expectations, or having a warm-up to start off class. "Reset buttons" are multiple new rules, expectations, and/or procedures that are so altering that students must be notified of them.

You can hit your "reset button" after a holiday break, after a three-day weekend, on a Monday. In secondary schools there may be natural opportunities with a new grading period or semester which may involve different students in the class. It does not matter, as long as you have taken the time to really reflect on what changes are needed. When you reset, you should reset *everything* that is not working, since this may be your only chance to do these alterations, and you *cannot* blame any of it on your students. When you hit the reset button, you want a "fresh start." If you start this new phase with, "You guys have been so terrible," is it really giving you and your students this new beginning?

> When you reset, you should reset *everything* that is not working, since this may be your only chance to do these alterations, and you *cannot* blame any of it on your students.

Here is how you hit your "reset button."

Identify the Issues

The first thing you have to do is identify the real issue. What is happening in your classroom that is not working for you? If you are elementary you need to figure out if the entire day is a disaster or if it is just the afternoon? Are students focused and on-task during free-write time but bouncing off the walls during math circles? Identify the exact times and places where you can no longer teach and your students can no longer learn. At the secondary level you need to decide whether or not every class/hour/period is struggling or if it is just one or two of them. Maybe your honors classes are always on task, but your regular 7th grade science classes cannot effectively function under the same rules and procedures.

Once you have pinpointed the times that you can no longer teach and your students can no longer learn you have to figure out why. Identify the behaviors you do not like and think through why they are happening. You may come up with a list of things that are not going well, or just one thing that needs major adjustment. For example, let's say that you feel your whole fourth hour is out of control. After serious reflection and observation, however, you realize that the issues actually stem from two things: students getting out of their seat at any time during the lesson, and students working on and turning in make-up work. Before, you did not realize that students getting out of their seats whenever they wanted was going to be an issue, but now students are distracting the entire class by dunking their trash into the trashcan 14 times each hour. Also, you never thought 10th graders would have trouble turning in late work and make-up assignments. Now you realize, though, that these issues are hindering your ability to be an effective teacher and things are just going to get worse unless you change something soon.

Decide on Necessary Changes

At this point, you might want to go back and read through the classroom procedures and classroom management chapters again. You might be thinking, "I already did that. I had a clear vision, a clear plan, and you helped me develop it." What makes this time different is that now you have your own students. Now you know yourself better as a teacher. Now you know your tolerance level when it comes to behavior or noise.

Thus, begin to ask yourself questions. Is there a procedure you are missing, or you need to introduce? Is there an expectation you said you had, but you are not reinforcing? Are there additional classroom rules that you add or take away? Your situation may sound like one of these or not, but no matter what it is, make sure you make a game-plan for how to fix it, based on what your students' misbehaviors are stemming from.

Going back to our example, we decided that the two major issues were students getting out of their seat during the lesson, and a lack of procedures around late and make-up work. Thus, one appropriate adjustment would be to add a new classroom rule called "Raise your hand to leave your seat." This teacher also needs to decide what will be done when a student does not follow this rule, if implementing consistent consequences has also been a problem. Another adjustment that should be made is around late and make-up work, so the teacher creates clear procedures for students who miss school or must turn in late work, that do not interrupt the beginning of the class time.

Implement Your New Vision

Once you have a new classroom vision, you might have new expectations. You might have new rules. You might have new procedures. You might have a mixture of all three. You have taken time to identify the issues and you are ready to recreate your classroom into the classroom you want it to be and the classroom it needs to be so your students can learn. Make sure you spent careful time coming up with this vision, because you can only push the "reset button" once (maybe twice). But do not be afraid of it not working perfectly—remember you can always tweak.

Now let's push the "reset button." This is a big moment, so you must come in fully prepared. Remember, this reset can take place on a Monday or a Friday. It may make more sense after a long weekend or holiday break, but it does not matter as long as you have thought through everything extensively, and you introduce and execute it correctly and with confidence. No matter the rules, procedures, or expectations you introduce, they must be upheld by *you* through your actions.

It is a Monday. You spent the entire weekend planning your new classroom. You reread certain sections of the book with your more experienced lens. You have explicitly written out the new expectations, procedures, and/or rules. You have thought through how you are going to uphold them. You know you are going to compliment students doing things the way you want them done. You know you are going to redirect those not following the new expectations immediately. You are ready to introduce this to your students.

Right when they walk in, you start the class off by introducing and explaining the changes you are making. Here is an example of the language you can use. "I was thinking this weekend about our class and decided it was time to improve our learning environment. I have come up with some new procedures and am so excited to introduce them. I want to make it so we can all work together and make sure everyone has the best learning experience they can. So here is what I came up with ..." At this point you would introduce the changes.

What is important about the language above is that you are excited, and have unwavering confidence about the future. Before the reset, you may have been really frustrated with your students' behavior, but when processing the issues that were occurring, you remembered whose fault it is. There is no need to even mention their previous behavior or place any blame on them. You all are a team and you want to work with them to be successful. Barely address the past and quickly move to fixing things for a better future.

Now that you have introduced the reset to students you have to maintain it. To maintain the reset you have to uphold the new procedures and expectations. Stay strong no matter what. The students will try to resort back to their old behavior or ways of doing things. You have to make sure you address each situation, redirect quickly, and have consequences in place if need be. Consistency is key.

The following are a few examples of how to uphold your new expectations.

1. The day of the reset you say that students will no longer shout out answers during the lesson. If they have something to say, whether it be an answer or a question, they must raise their hand. Five minutes into the lesson, you pose a question and Jaleya shouts out the correct answer. You MUST address this. "Jaleya, I love that you knew the correct answer, but this does not follow our new expectations, can you try that again?" Force her to raise her hand, call on her, and thank her for raising her hand and giving the correct answer.

2. Let's say a few minutes later you pose a question, 15 students raise their hands, but you still have three students shout out answers. Praise and ignore. "George, thank you so much for raising your hand! What are your thoughts?"

3. By the end of the lesson most students have caught on, but you realize that Anthony is still shouting out. With about a minute left in class, walk up to him, lean down, and say, "Please stay after class so we can have a quick chat." Once the students have left, you need to have a serious conversation about his continual shouting out. "Anthony, I noticed you were struggling to follow our new procedure. I know raising your hand can be hard, especially when you

are confident about your answers, but when you do that you are interrupting other students' thinking processes. Tomorrow I will give you one warning, but if you shout out an answer twice in the period you are going to have to go to a buddy room. Do you have any questions about this?" We know removing Anthony for not raising his hand seems extreme, but this is a change that must be made so you can teach and the students can learn. Do not forget, your classroom was out of control. You have to be overly serious about these changes so students take them seriously. The next day before class you need to stop Anthony before he enters the room. "Anthony, please do not forget to raise your hand today. I want you to be able to stay in class so I can hear your thoughts and correct answers!"

If you can uphold this reset for a solid two weeks things will begin to run like clockwork. You may have to be more stern and serious than you prefer to be, but you have to sacrifice for a while so you can teach and your students can learn. Remember you can always soften your expectations but it is quite difficult to ratchet them tighter.

It is critical to remember that you can only push the "reset button" once (maybe twice) a year. It is a powerful tool, but each time you use it, it becomes less and less powerful. If you "reset" once, students will take it seriously. You are changing the entire structure of your classroom: That is a big deal. It is almost like students getting an entirely new class. If you "reset" a second time students are going to wonder why you keep changing it up. The third time you openly "reset" is almost a joke. Push the "reset button" with careful thought and preparation!

> **It is critical to remember that you can only push the "reset button" once (maybe twice) a year.**

15

Be a Sponge

Soak It Up

As a first year teacher, everything is new: meetings, teams, curriculum, teacher interactions, student interactions, etc. Try to view every single situation at school as an opportunity to learn. Take your time the first year to absorb everything; be a sponge.

Observing Others

One way you can put yourself into a "soak it up" situation is by using your plan time as an opportunity to watch other teachers teach. Observe how they start class, how they end class, how they transition between activities. Listen carefully to the language they use when interacting with their students. How do they redirect behavior? Just because you now have your own classroom does not necessarily mean you are done observing other teachers. Figuring out how your peers navigate the school and the clientele can be truly insightful. Secondary teachers can learn a lot from elementary teachers and vice versa.

For example, a secondary middle school teacher once observed a kindergarten classroom walk in a perfectly straight line silently down the hallway. He was in shock. If you are elementary, you know what a struggle that is! Actually, if you are any level, you know what a struggle it is to create a straight, silent line. Every time he saw that class, he watched and listened to the teacher. One day he finally learned her secret. The class was standing, waiting for their turn to go up the stairs, when one student decided he wanted to touch the person's hair in front of him. The teacher saw him and all she said was, "Cortez, I am so sorry you made that choice." He immediately put his head down. Truth be told, the secondary teacher said he also wanted to hang his head in shame because of the one time he had touched someone's hair back in 2nd grade. If that sentence made a kindergartener feel guilty (and an adult who had not even done anything wrong feel guilty), he thought it had to work on his students. He was right. Small observations like that can truly change the way you think about things.

Attending Meetings

A second situation where you can absorb knowledge is during meetings. Be sure to listen to your peers and leaders, because, as we have mentioned previously, you can learn so much from the experts who surround you. During these times, if you do not understand something, do not be afraid to either ask for clarification during the meetings or write your questions down and ask a colleague or supervisor later. They understandably may not realize or remember the giant learning curve first year teachers have to go through. As teachers, we tell our students that there is never a dumb question. The truth still holds true as adults. Just because you are now a teacher

> There are times you are going to feel more like a student than a teacher and there is nothing wrong with that. Embrace it. It is better to ask questions or for clarification than pretend to know it all.

does not mean you have all the answers. There are times you are going to feel more like a student than a teacher and there is nothing wrong with that. Embrace it. It is better to ask questions or for clarification than pretend to know it all. Not even the veteran teachers in your building, or even your principals, know it all.

Be Observed Yourself

As a new teacher, one of the best ways to truly get better is to be observed and given feedback. You may end up in a school that already has structures in place to make sure you are regularly observed. If this is not the case, it may be beneficial for you to ask to be observed by the principal, a colleague, or a trusted peer. This may seem scary at first, but what if there is a better way to start your class that you haven't thought of? What if you are so focused on the content of your lesson that you fail to realize the kids in the back are not attentive? What if there was a better way to quickly assess student learning? Wouldn't you want to know these things? Don't you want to be the best you can be?

As a final note, if there are specific things you want help with or advice on, it may be helpful to let the person observing you know. They will make sure to pay attention to that instead of other things you are not as worried about. Now, once you get people to observe you, you need to be open to all the feedback they give you. You may not agree with every part of it, and that is okay, but hearing different perspectives will always make you better. Everyone will have different ideas, suggestions, and techniques for you to try. Do not let yourself be afraid of feedback. This can potentially be one of the best ways to improve.

Don't Be Afraid to Say No

Finally, take this next piece of "sponge" advice seriously: *do not over work yourself.* If opportunities to try new things arise, we encourage you to explore them. Join new committees. Volunteer to work those events after school. Be willing to stretch outside of your classroom. It is an amazing way to better understand how your school works and to meet and interact with new people. As first year teachers it is unbelievably hard to say "no," for two reasons. The first being that you are so excited! You want to please, you want to be around kids, and you want to be great. This is all why you wanted to become a teacher. The second reason it is hard to say "no" is that you are not quite sure you are allowed to. Will people be mad at me if I say no? Will my principal think I am a slacker because I cannot lesson plan, keep grades updated, and serve on four committees?

You have to do what is best for you. You also have to do what is best for your students. These two things are very much connected. The other educators in the building will get it. As long as you are putting students first, nothing else matters. Do not be afraid to get involved in things outside of the classroom, but do not be afraid to say no if things get overwhelming. You will know what is best for you.

> **Do not be afraid to get involved in things outside of the classroom, but do not be afraid to say no if things get overwhelming. You will know what is best for you.**

Just as you can over-commit outside of the classroom, you can also do the same thing in your classroom. As a teacher, it can sometimes seem like your to-do list may never end. You cross one thing off then add three more. As a first year teacher it is almost worse, because you have not sorted out what is worthy of the to-do list yet. You cross off one thing then literally add 30 more things, because everything seems important when you are a first year teacher. Thus, focus on simplification. For example, your grading system. Is there a way for you to simplify it so you are not over-committing inside your classroom?

Examples of this could include:

1. Not grading every single piece of homework you assign
2. Making sure the homework you assign is actually necessary
3. Having students grade their own homework in pen then turn it into you
4. While students are doing a warm-up, walking around with a roster and clipboard to check their homework and only give it a completion grade
5. Finding ways to give quizzes or parts of tests on the computer so it automatically grades it for you.

Are there jobs you can assign to your students during the day to help ease your load after school?

Examples of this could include utilizing your students to:

1. Pass out papers (graded homework, note sheets, worksheets)
2. Set up activities (gather materials for their groups, cut out cards themselves)
3. Organize shelves in the classroom
4. Operate your classroom Twitter account
5. Collect materials after an activity (glue bottles, scissors, etc.)
6. Pick up items off the floor
7. Sharpen pencils.

At some point you have to give yourself permission to leave. Your to-do list will never be empty, and the quicker you become okay with that, the better off you will be. If you do not take care of yourself, your ability to take care of your students is much more limited. Make sure that you treat yourself physically and mentally to an appropriate balance. The students deserve the best you there is.

16

It Always Starts with You

Teaching is so fascinating. We can think about the impact of the principal in a school or visualize the influence that previous teachers have had on our students. We might hear people comment on the state legislature or state board of education and how they are affecting the profession. We might hear conversations related to the superintendent, central office, or school board and how what they do impacts teachers in your school. Yet, being honest, the most important person in that classroom is the teacher. Always has been, always will be.

It would be nice if every student who was in our classes came from a loving and stable home. It would be wonderful if every student read at or above grade level and loved school to their core. We can hope that each student this year has a wonderful attitude and disposition. We can hope that our salary is tripled and our class size is cut in half. Yet not only do we know these things are not likely, we know they are not possible.

If great teachers give a quiz or a test and the students do poorly on it, who do they blame? Of course, themselves. That is why they are so good. Whose is the one person's behavior we actually have the ability to control and influence? Our own.

Conversely, if ineffective teachers give a quiz or a test and the students do poorly on it, who do they blame? Last year's teachers, the parents, Netflix, twerking, society today, the divorce rate, etc. If we are looking for someone else or something else to change, we may feel quite frustrated, helpless, and even hopeless our entire life. However, if we realize it is really us, versus something out of our control, we now have hope. It can be scary to realize it is up to us, but it can also be very empowering.

Too often teachers who say, "This is the worst group of students I have ever had!" have said it every year on a corresponding date. What they are really saying is that they will start teaching again as soon as someone brings them better students. It sounds silly when we think of others doing these things. It is important that we focus on ourselves as the key influence in the classroom.

Students typically misbehave because they are getting some kind of a reward for it. It might be attention of any type—laughter, anger, etc. And to be honest, they usually get that attention from the teacher. Classroom management has a lot more to do with class than it does management. In most schools, there are teachers who never yell, and there are teachers who yell on a consistent basis. Which teacher do you want to be? It is your choice.

When you are unhappy with a lesson or displeased with student behavior, run to the bathroom and look in the mirror. That is the only place to find the answer. Teaching is a tremendous responsibility. Teaching is a tremendous opportunity. How you deal with both is up to you.

Teaching is a tremendous responsibility. Teaching is a tremendous opportunity. How you deal with both is up to you.

Trust Your Gut

The last section reminded us how teaching and what happens in the classroom on a daily basis is up to us—the teacher. It's really weird—teaching is one of the loneliest professions that there is and yet we are never alone. There are usually 20–30-plus students in that classroom with us and yet in terms of peer adults, seldom does anyone see us and too seldom does anyone provide us the specific guidance we may need. That is the reason we wrote this section. Do not be afraid to rely on your instincts. Do not be afraid to trust your gut.

You may have an occasion where you feel like the students are taking advantage of you. You are probably right. You might have a time where you wondered if you spoke too harshly to your class or an individual student. You are probably correct. There may be a time that you feel like a particular assignment didn't make sense, you were not clear in your explanation, or your tone was sarcastic. You were probably right, right, and right.

You chose to be a teacher because you want to have a positive impact. You chose the right profession. Believe in yourself. Don't be afraid to apologize if you feel like you crossed the line. Feel free, in a professional manner, to share with a student that they are behaving inappropriately. And, don't fret if you did not get in touch with your instincts immediately. There is nothing wrong with pondering about it overnight or even mulling it over for a few days and then taking an alternate approach.

There is no one else who is going to be in your classroom giving you guidance on a regular basis. Rely on your instincts. If you are unsure and your instinct tells you to ask someone with more experience, do that also. There is no *always* or only one right answer. Do not be afraid to look inside yourself and trust what you find to help guide you on a daily basis.

> There is no *always* or only one right answer. Do not be afraid to look inside yourself and trust what you find to help guide you on a daily basis.

Just because a colleague yells or uses sarcasm does not make it correct. When other teachers are eating lunch and being critical of the principal, you should not feel the need to join in on the bashing party. Many times when we do things like this we may be reinforced immediately because a student behaves for a few minutes because we yelled or some of our peers laugh when we make fun of a colleague or administrator behind their back. But after reflection we feel bad that we did it. Your gut is telling you this was inappropriate. This was unprofessional. At times we should repair. At all times we should choose a different behavior in the future. Part of teaching is learning. Part of teaching is teaching ourselves.

17

What's Next?

Before you start your first year as a teacher, you spend time envisioning and dreaming about the kind of teacher you want to be. These dreams continue to grow up until the first day you are with your students. From then on you work hard to be that teacher you envisioned. We all hope to be that person from day one; however, many of us find it harder than we originally thought it would be. That mental list of things you said you would never do may start to slowly trickle its way into your practices.

You swore you were never going to primarily use lecture as an instructional practice to your students. Yet here you are, two months into the school year, making students sit and take notes all hour. You swore you would never yell at a student, but when Lilly starts rolling around on the floor for the fourth time that day, you find your patience at its limit.

Although the first year will not be perfect, that does not mean you have failed as a teacher. Everything that happens is an opportunity to learn, grow, and work toward becoming the teacher you dreamed of.

At the end of the day you sit at your desk and think about the teacher you wanted to be and who you actually were that day. Did you fail? Is that teacher you dreamed about being ever going to show up? Is this person really who you have become? Although the first year will not be perfect, that does not mean you have failed as a teacher. Everything that happens is an opportunity to learn, grow, and work toward becoming the teacher you dreamed of.

It is possible to become that vision but you may have to work at it. The point is to never give up on making that dream a reality. If you feel yourself starting to slip away from who you want to be, fix it. Never just accept the negative change that you feel happening. If you catch yourself becoming a lecturer when you swore you would never be that, fix it. Be creative. Find different ways to present the material. Do not be afraid to make a change. If you are blanketed by a wave of regret after you yelled at a student for the first time, instead of wallowing in regret, figure out how to repair and decide what you will do differently next time.

Do not let situations like these discourage your professional teaching journey. These instances will help you grow and constantly become better. Remember, we teach our students to be fearless in their learning, and you should too. The best teachers are the best learners. You *can* be that dream teacher. Do not put it off until next year, because this year's students deserve that dream teacher now.

You'll Start Year Two Undefeated

In most professions there is a not a clear start and end to a professional year. If you work in an office, it is typically just one continuous cycle. If you start your job there on the wrong foot, you may never recover. Your clients are your clients, and it is really difficult to reboot even if we wish we could. Luckily you are not in another profession. You are in the best profession—teaching. And though the school year cycle may cause great stress at times— the anxiousness of the next holiday, worry about standardized testing, curriculum expectations, etc.—there is one benefit for new employees that other jobs do not have. And that is the start of a new school year.

The end of your first year is a wonderful time to self-reflect, full of celebrations but also regrets. You may have wished you had established clearer expectations at the beginning of the year. Maybe you didn't repair as often as you wished you had. Most likely some lessons did not go as well as you had hoped or had imagined. Maybe you had to do a couple of resets and they were too late to have the impact you wanted. Well, there is hope on the horizon: year two! No matter how your first year went, you start year two undefeated. From day one, you now have the opportunity to treat every student with respect, you have the knowledge to design engaging and culturally relevant lessons, you have the confidence to be a consistent and positive influence for your school.

No matter how your first year went, you start year two undefeated. From day one, you now have the opportunity to treat every student with respect, you have the knowledge to design engaging and culturally relevant lessons, you have the confidence to be a consistent and positive influence for your school.

There may be parts of the book you want to revisit as the new year gets closer. The anticipation of a new year is always exciting. No matter how year one went, next year's students will walk into your classroom with excitement and hope. They have been waiting all summer to have a teacher like you. And you have been waiting all summer to have students like them. Have a great second year.

References

Beaty-O'Ferrall, M. E., Green, A., & Hanna, F. (March 2010). Classroom Management Strategies for Difficult Students: Promoting Change through Relationships. *Middle School Journal, 41 (4)*, 4–11.

Chang, M.-L. (2009). An Appraisal Perspective of Teacher Burnout: Examining the Emotional Work of Teachers. *Educational Psychology Review, 21*, 193–218.

Cornelius-White, J. (2007). Learner-Centered Teacher–Student Relationships Are Effective: A Meta-Analysis. *Review of Educational Research, 77 (1)*, 113–143.

Dweck, C. S. (2006). *Mindset: The New Psychology of Success.* New York: Ballantine Books.

Emmer, E. T. & Saborine, E. J. (2015). *Handbook of Classroom Management, 2nd Edition*. New York: Routledge Publishing Company.

Fay, J. & Funk, D. (1995). *Teaching with Love and Logic.* Golden, CO: The Love and Logic Press.

Fredricks, J. A., Blumenfeld, P. C., & Paris, A. H. (2004). School Engagement: Potential of the Concept, State of the Evidence. *Review of Educational Research, 74 (1)*, 59–109.

Friedman, I. A. (2006). Classroom Management and Teacher Stress and Burnout. In C. M. Evertson & C. S. Weinstein (Eds.), *Handbook of Classroom Management: Research, Practice, and Contemporary Issues* (925–944). Mahwah, NJ: Erlbaum.

Hamre, B. K. & Pianta, R. C. (2006). Student–Teacher Relationships. In G. G. Bear & K. M. Minke (Eds.), *Children's Needs III: Development, Prevention and Intervention* (59–71). Bathesda, MD: National Association of School Psychologists.

Jones, F. (2013). *Tools for Teaching: Discipline, Instruction, Motivation, 3rd Edition.* Santa Cruz, CA: Fredric H. Jones & Associates Inc.

Kearney, K. & McCroskey, J. C. (1980). Relationships among Teacher Communication Style, Trait and State Communication

Apprehension and Teacher Effectiveness. In D. Nimmo (Ed.), *Communication Yearbook 4* (533–551). New Brunswick, NJ: Transaction Books.

Klassen, R. M. & Chiu, M. M. (2010). Effects on Teachers' Self-Efficacy and Job Satisfaction: Teacher Gender, Years of Experience, and Job Stress. *Journal of Educational Psychology, 102 (3)*, 741–756.

Kuzsman, F. L. & Schnall, H. (1987). Managing Teachers' Stress: Improving Discipline. *The Canadian School Executive*, 6, 3–10.

Maag, J. W. (2001). Rewarded by Punishment: Reflections on the Disuse of Positive Reinforcement in Schools. *Exceptional Children, 67 (2)*, 173–186.

Marks, H. M. (2000). Student Engagement in Instructional Activity: Patterns in the Elementary, Middle and High School Years. *American Educational Research Journal, 37 (1)*, 153–184.

Marzano, R. J., Gaddy, B. B., Foseid, M. C., Foseid, M. P., & Marzano, J. S. (2005). *A Handbook for Classroom Management that Works*. Alexandria, VA: Association for Supervision and Curriculum Development.

Newmann, F. M., Wehlage, G. G., & Lamborn S. D. (1992). Chapter One: The Significance and Sources of Student Engagement. In F. M. Newmann (Ed.), *Student Engagement and Achievement in American Secondary Schools* (11–39). New York: Teachers College, Columbia University.

Roorda, D. L., Koomen, H. M. Y., Spilt, J. L., & Oort, F. J. (2011). The Influence of Affective Teacher–Student Relationships on Students' School Engagement and Achievement: A Meta-analytic Approach. *Review of Educational Research, 81 (4)*, 493–529.

Savage, T. V. & Savage, M. K. (2009). *Successful Classroom Management and Discipline: Teaching Self Control and Responsibility, 3rd Edition*. Thousand Oaks, CA: SAGE Publications.

Scott, S. (2004). *Fierce Conversations: Achieving Success at Work and in Life One Conversation at a Time*. Berkeley, CA: Berkeley Publishing Group.

Wang, M. C., Haertel, G. D., & Walberg, H. J. (1993). Toward a Knowledge Base for School Learning. *Review of Educational Research, 63 (3)*, 249–294.

Wasicisko, M. M. & Ross, S. M. (1994). How to Create Discipline Problems. *The Clearing House*, May/June. Washington D. C.: Heldref Publications. (In K. Ryan & J. M. Cooper (Eds.), *Kaleidoscope: Contemporary and Classic Readings in Education, 12th Edition* (62–66). Belmont, CA: Wadsworth Cengage Learning (2010).)

Whitaker, T. (2012). *What Great Teachers Do Differently, 2nd Edition*. New York: Routledge.

Whitaker, T. & Fiore, D. (2016). *Dealing with Difficult Parents, 2nd Edition*. New York: Routledge.